Transforming Schools: Illusion or Reality

Bernard Barker

Trentham books

Stoke on Trent, UK and Sterling, USA

UNIVERSITY OF CHICHESTER

Trentham Books Limited
Westview House   22883 Quicksilver Drive
734 London Road   Sterling
Oakhill   VA 20166-2012
Stoke on Trent   USA
Staffordshire
England ST4 5NP

© 2005 Bernard Barker

First published 2005

British Library Cataloguing-in-Publication Data
A catalogue record for this book is available from the British
Library

ISBN-13: 978-1-85856-364-0
ISBN-10: 1-85856-364-X

Designed and typeset by Trentham Print Design Ltd, Chester and
printed in Great Britain by The Cromwell Press Ltd, Wiltshire.

Contents

For Ann and Irena

Acknowledgements

I have tried to describe comprehensive schools as they were in my time (1971–2001) through the eyes and ears of the parents, teachers and children at Hillside as they struggled against the odds for meaning, identity and survival. If I have failed to do justice to their experience, it is not their fault and I wish to record my admiration and thanks to them for allowing me to share their adventure and accepting my research as another quirk in a peculiar world.

My warmest thanks are due to my colleagues and students at the School of Education, University of Leicester, who have explained why it is so difficult to investigate social organisations, while showing forbearance during my more excitable and overbearing moments. Maurice Galton introduced me to the scholarly world of education; Tom Whiteside reminded me of the sociological perspective; Ken Fogelman helped me through the thorniest problems; Les Bell enabled me see the project through.

My wife Ann has accepted my escapism with resignation but her love and friendship, always informed by practical common sense and unwavering honesty, has sustained us both through triumphs and disasters that we have tried to treat just the same. I began in friendly competition with our son Chris, whose doctoral thesis at Imperial College on *Calluna vulgaris* owes rather more to quantitative methods than my own, so now my inexpressible regret is that I have to imagine his gentle mockery of this subjective enquiry. Our daughter, Irena, is less than enthusiastic about schools but she is a wise confidante who tries to help with my weaknesses: 'you try too hard at everything, Dad'.

And finally, my father, who proof-read my history thesis in 1971, is around to take an interest in this belated effort. How can I thank my parents for believing in me for so long and for giving me an enduring faith in the life-changing, life-enhancing importance of education?

Bernard Barker, April 2005

Abbreviations

CAT	Cognitive Ability Test
CV	Curriculum vitae
DfEE	Department for Education and Employment
GCSE	General Certificate of Secondary Education
GMS	Grant Maintained School
HMI	Her Majesty's Inspector(s) of Schools
ICT	Information and Communication Technology
IQEA	Improving the Quality of Education for All
ISIP	International School Improvement Project
KS	Key Stage
LEA	Local Education Authority
LMS	Local Management of Schools
LPSH	Leadership Programme for Serving Headteachers
MP	Member of Parliament
NAS/UWT	National Association of Schoolmasters/Union of Women Teachers
NCSL	National College of School Leadership
NPQH	National Professional Qualification for Headship
NQT	Newly Qualified Teacher
Ofsted	Office for Standards in Education
PAG	Parents' Action Group
PE	Physical Education
RE	Religious Education
SAT	Standard Assessment Task
SEN	Special Educational Needs
SIMS	School Information Management Systems
SMT	Senior Management Team
TTA	Teacher Training Agency
UK	United Kingdom
US	United States

'Hillside' staff and students named in the text (All names are fictitious)

Name	Role
Alan	Retired Senior Teacher brought in to assist changes
Anne	Office Assistant, then Personal Assistant to the Head and SMT
Caretaker	
Chair of Governors	
Clive	PAG Chair; Governor
Darren	PE teacher; NQT
David Brown	Geography teacher
Di	Teacher
Donna	Temporary Senior Teacher
Doris	Office assistant
Elaine	Year Head, then Deputy Head
Eleanor	SEN teacher
George	Long-serving Technology teacher
Gerald	Bursar
Graham	Temporary Senior Teacher
Ian	Teacher
Jade	Troublesome student
Jean	Head of Year 10
Jeanne	New office manager
Jenny	Head of Humanities
John	Mathematics teacher
John	Student
Julian	Senior Teacher, responsible for Modern Languages
Katrina	Troublesome student

The head teachers are, in chronological order,

Albert Wake	Long-serving Head
Brian Goodlad	Acting Head (one term)
Chris Moore	Acting Head (two years)

Throughout the text they are referred to as they were in the school: as Mr Wake, Mr Goodlad and Mr Moore

Pam	Canteen Supervisor
Peter	Year Head, then Deputy Head
Sarah	Student
Sidney	Long-serving Senior Teacher; Head of Lower School
Stephen	Head of Careers
Tracey	Student
William	RE teacher

During this transformation the forest moves with a speed greater than that of animals, for animals do not grow as fast as plants; yet this movement cannot be observed. The forest does not change its place, we cannot lie in wait for it and catch it in the act of moving. However much we look at it we see it as motionless. And such also is the immobility to our eyes of the eternally growing, ceaselessly changing life of society, of history moving as invisibly in its incessant transformations as the forest in spring.

Doctor Zhivago, Boris Pasternak, 1958

1

Introduction

Hillside School's descent into special measures and the transformation that followed are at the centre of this book. An ethnographic narrative of decline, fall and resurgence captures the details of disaster and recreates the drama of survival and escape. As parents, teachers and children learned to fight back, unexpected heroes appeared to play their parts in an epic campaign to outwit the Ofsted thought police and save the school from closure. Ordinary families and teachers were the main actors in the events that unfolded and their thoughts and feelings have informed the account presented in chapters three to six. This is their tale. It could be told from numerous perspectives, each with its dominant voices and concerns. The book in your hands, however, is written by an outsider. I turned up with beliefs and assumptions that have influenced my portrayal of events at Hillside, despite my methodological self-awareness and determination to strive for objectivity. As a former head, I was eager to research the impact of headteachers on school culture and organisation. Could leaders transform their schools?

The rise of leadership

The arrival of a new government in 1997 stimulated a renewed and sustained interest in leadership as a major theme in education policy, so my enquiry became more relevant and significant than I had intended. Blunkett (2000) and Blair (2001) stressed the role of

1

leaders and leadership in transforming schools and provided the impetus for the invention of the National College of School Leadership (NCSL) in November 2000 (Bolam, 2004). Although the NCSL inherited standards and programmes developed initially by the Teacher Training Agency (TTA), the creation of a single national focus for leadership has contributed to the emergence of a new and pervasive policy agenda. Leaders at all levels are expected to motivate and empower their colleagues by following models of excellence that are believed to have the potential to produce remarkable improvements in school performance (NCSL, 2003).

The expectation that strong leaders can turn schools round quickly seemed to be confirmed by the experience of the 250 schools placed in special measures by January 1997. Half of the incumbent heads were replaced, either shortly before or after failing an Ofsted inspection. Under new management, the schools built a common purpose and secured appropriate improvement (Stark, 1998). Apparently successful quick fixes encouraged the government's reluctance to tolerate failure (Barber, 1998) and created a climate where local authorities and governors in the UK were actively searching for exceptional leaders to deal with failing schools like Hillside. Special measures became a crucible for experiments in transformational leadership.

The available empirical evidence, however, does not justify this transformational agenda. Faith in the power of visionary leaders to improve effectiveness and results is widespread but we lack longitudinal and observational studies of schools where leadership has produced the expected gains in performance (Hall and Southworth, 1997). Although heads have written personal accounts of rescue missions at failing schools (Dawson, 1981, Clark, 1998), empirical studies of leaders engaging with reform are rare. None of the twelve schools investigated by Gray *et al* (1999) managed to consolidate a higher position in the league table. A wide range of studies indicates that leadership effects are indirect and small (Earley and Evans, 2004).

The yawning gulf between government expectations and the limited results detected in the schools suggests that we should be cautious about claims that transformational leaders improve motivation and enhance performance (Fullan, 2003, Goleman *et al*, 2003). We need observational, qualitative studies of heads leading change to explain the discrepancy between the widespread belief that leaders make an important difference and the lack of convincing evidence that their impact on school effectiveness is significant.

These considerations prompted me to approach Hillside as a case study in transformational leadership (Barker, 2003). *Transforming Schools* explores how two successive acting headteachers led a struggling small comprehensive in the Midlands through special measures and considers the implications of their journey for everyone who hopes to transform the quality and performance of schools in this country. Theoretical models of leadership are tested against the experience of headteachers in the field. Can transformational leaders stimulate a dramatic change in efficiency and effectiveness that produces a lasting improvement in results? Do the models developed by the NCSL offer a practical, reproducible formula for transformation?

Named and shamed

The story begins one dark December evening when the Hillside governors gathered in the library to hear the registered inspector's oral report. Ofsted had inspected the eleven to sixteen, co-educational, multicultural comprehensive two weeks earlier and everyone at the meeting was anxious to learn how they had done.

The inspection team's verdict was damning.

> *The progress that significant numbers of pupils make is unsatisfactory.*

> *Progress is judged to be unsatisfactory in almost 40% of lessons.*

> *The quality of teaching varies widely across the school.*

> *The leadership provided by the headteacher and governing body is ineffective as it does not promote high expectations or take a strategic view of the need to improve standards.*

> *Pupils can be poorly behaved and restless. Teachers, by their attitude, provoke bad behaviour.*

It is our judgement that the school should be placed in special measures.

For the governors assembled that evening, especially the teachers, this was 'shell shock night'. Albert Wake, the long-serving head-teacher, had been debriefed at the end of the inspection and knew that Hillside had been recommended for special measures but had decided to keep the information to himself. After this formal reading of the inspection report, however, there was no prospect of containing the damage or controlling the consequences. The published report named and shamed Mr Wake and the governors and placed Hillside amongst the two per cent of schools nationally deemed to be failing (Fitz *et al*, 2000).

Easton, the newly formed unitary authority responsible for the school, reacted at once to the special measures judgement by announcing that Hillside would close as part of a plan to reduce the number of surplus places in the city. Parents, governors and teachers were stung into an immediate and energetic response. An action group was formed and campaigned to save the school. The governors recruited two acting heads to provide the energy and leadership needed to restore the school's credibility. Brian Goodlad was seconded from a neighbouring school for one term and embarked on the radical actions necessary for survival. Chris Moore, a retired headteacher, then accepted a two-year contract to complete the job.

The Hillside case study

When I learned of these dramatic events I saw the opportunity to investigate leadership in circumstances generally considered suitable for rapid transformation. I hoped to complete a detailed ethnographic case study of the school as it struggled to transform itself so I volunteered to become a participant researcher. Governors, parents and teachers were eager to have their struggle for survival recorded and readily accepted my offer.

My research ran for two full academic years and covered actions and events over three school years. I organised a disordered mass of documentary material into eighteen folders. The result is a detailed record of actions and events through the life of the study. The folders contain copies of all the school's new policies, systems and procedures, the action plan, progress reports, lesson transcripts and other records relevant to the study. A considerable but incomplete archive of documents has also survived for the period between Hillside's opening and the first Ofsted inspection. Five Ofsted reports, including four prepared by HMI, provide external confirmation of the school's progress.

Mr Moore gave access to his diary, written during his first year as acting principal and running to over 300,000 words. Written mostly in the present tense, the main narrative is descriptive and chronological, capturing and commenting on fast-flowing daily events as they happen. Day-by-day reportage is punctuated by reflection, argument and speculation. Passionately expressed opinions are balanced by passages exploring alternative interpretations and points of view. Conversations with colleagues are reported and interpreted. The diary is a rare, detailed contemporary record and gives direct access to the head's own intentions and perspectives.

As a participant researcher, I observed students, staff and governors in a variety of contexts, including classrooms, was involved in frequent conversations with school and community members, attended numerous meetings and conducted six formal and many informal interviews with teachers and children. Transcripts of the formal interviews were prepared from tape recordings; notes of the informal interviews were typed from memory later in the day. Interviews lasted approximately one hour.

Over two years, a university colleague conducted 29 semi-structured, tape-recorded interviews, each lasting approximately 45 minutes. Ten key witnesses were selected to reflect the perspectives of different status positions within the school. Because time was limited, no students or parents were interviewed, although two staff members included on other grounds were also parents of children at the school. Of the original ten participants, only five remained by the end of the research. One new participant was recruited during the life of the project. The views and opinions quoted in chapters three to six are derived from interview transcripts or typed notes of informal contacts and discussion.

All the interviews conducted by the external researcher were transcribed and checked, except in cases where participants declined the opportunity to verify their contributions, usually because they felt uncomfortable reading their own words. The external researcher completed an analysis of the transcripts independently and withheld access to the data until my own involvement with Hillside was concluded and there was no danger of the information divulged in the research context influencing the internal processes of the school. The combination of participant research, the document archive, the acting head's diary and external interviews, conducted by someone whose objectivity was not compromised by active involvement in the school, enabled me to compare and contrast multiple sources of evidence with an exceptional degree of objectivity (Denscombe, 1983).

Chapters three to six blend these primary sources together in a continuous narrative that is centred on the processes of change and improvement. Analysis of the resulting evidence is inductive and uses theoretical concepts and frameworks from the leadership literature to interpret unfolding behaviour and events. There is a high level of internal agreement in the recall, description and interpretation of events. The people who appear in the narrative are represented as fully, fairly and truthfully as possible so that their dignity and privacy are respected (Pring, 2000). Names, places and other details have been changed or adapted so that none of those involved in the study may be identified. Dates have been omitted to reduce the risk of Hillside being recognised through the details of chronology. Particulars relating to the participant researcher have been withheld to further protect the anonymity of the school.

Significance and scope
Although a single case study cannot in itself validate or refute the models of leadership developed by government agencies, especially the NCSL, Hillside does provide a 'critical test of existing theory' (Yin, 1994, p44) about how schools in special measures are turned round. NCSL leadership programmes are considered equally suitable for heads of schools of all sizes and types, while government recommendations for schools in general (firm leadership, action plans, challenging targets and systematic monitoring) are supposed

to be particularly appropriate for institutions in special measures (Stark, 1998). Hillside is therefore a suitable setting for a theory-seeking, theory-testing case study designed to produce 'a fuzzy generalisation' (Bassey, 1999) about the relevance and usefulness of government models. Descriptions based on detailed evidence gathered at Hillside have the potential to reveal fresh perspectives on leadership and change. There are inevitable risks in drawing general conclusions from a small number of studies but the depth and richness of material explored in a single case enable particular problems and issues to be observed and give access over time to groups and processes that would otherwise remain invisible (Gomm *et al*, 2000).

Hillside has, therefore, the potential to confirm or qualify our understanding of transformational leadership, at least in the specific context of special measures. The two new heads set out to:

- re-motivate demoralised teachers (NCSL, 2003)

- rebuild the school's culture and organisation (Schein, 2004)

- build capacity (Hopkins, 2000)

- create detailed development plans (Ofsted, 1994)

- set challenging targets (DfEE, 1998)

- transform Hillside's effectiveness (Blair, 2001)

Evidence that a 'failing' school was transformed as the model pre-dicts would help justify current policy and would confirm the wis-dom of the best practice recommended by government agencies. Alternatively, indications that the prevailing performance paradigm has ignored the 'messy' nature of management and underestimates circumstantial constraints and contingencies should open space for enquiry beyond the current obsession with effectiveness and productivity.

The pursuit of quick fixes (Stoll and Myers, 1998) and unrealistic targets may have encouraged policy recommendations with a more limited application than is commonly supposed. The policy agenda in this country is driven by a sense of urgency that relates to the electoral cycle rather than the reality of schools (Barber, 1997). Six curriculum and assessment agencies have been created and abolished in twelve years, for example, and there were five Secretaries of State between 1997 and 2005. It may be more realistic to envisage a swamp where simple solutions do not work:

> ...the ground on which school leaders base their practices becomes increasingly swampy, as fewer and fewer of these conditions are met: the swamp is especially deep when one only vaguely understands the present situation, has no clear way of knowing what would be better, and lacks procedures for addressing obstacles or constraints. (Leithwood *et al*, 1992, p42)

Is transformational leadership a realistic proposition or is the swamp an inescapable constraint for all those who seek to improve our schools?

This study examines the development of an urgent contemporary policy agenda through the literature of school effectiveness, improvement and transformation (chapter two) and explores the processes of leadership and change at Hillside School (chapters three to six). The research data is analysed to test the validity of models identified in the literature and to inform a set of specific recommendations for all those concerned to learn from the case study experience and to improve their own schools (chapter seven). Finally, the nature of the changes at Hillside is evaluated – was the transformation an illusion or was it a reality (chapter eight)?

2

Improvement and Transformation

Although transformational leadership is a relatively recent element in the policy agenda, the concept itself is far from new. Smiles (1860) documented the personal qualities that helped heroes of the industrial revolution like Watt and Arkwright to achieve business success. Max Weber (1964) analysed the role of charismatic individuals who persuade their followers to adopt new attitudes and patterns of behaviour. Burns' classic study of transformational leaders and their methods and impact first appeared in 1978. American business schools have a long history of studying leadership and identifying the characteristics associated with outstanding performance (Peters, 1989).

In the UK, however, powerful cultural influences delayed the discovery of leadership as an important policy theme. Interest in effectiveness, improvement and management was slow to develop whilst politicians and educators were uncertain whether heads should become chief executives responsible for business administration or leading professionals who should change the classroom. This chapter examines our evolving conceptions of school leadership and improvement, from uncomplicated ideas about efficient management to the contemporary suggestion that transforming, distributed and instructional models should be combined to bring about large-scale, sustainable reform (Fullan, 2003).

Scientific management

The faith that leadership and management can improve efficiency, quality and performance has deep roots in the US. Since the early years of the twentieth century American reformers have tried to construct planned, bureaucratic systems of schooling that deliver predictable learning and maximum productivity. The monitorial system, distinguished by explicit rules and regimented behaviour, was intended to ensure that classroom learning was conducted effectively. Taylor (1911) stimulated an obsession with scientific management. Rational procedures were invented to improve every aspect of education, from teaching and learning to administration. Principals and teachers in the US were seen as managers and technicians whose job was to engineer the best possible results.

Cuban (1988) contrasts these technical, white-coated images with an alternative, craftsman-artist model of pedagogic leadership that retains its appeal for many teachers to this day, despite the periodic management mania that has shaped so much of American education. Humanistic versions of the classroom have been under continuous pressure, nevertheless. Scientific management became an article of faith during the New Deal and World War Two as experts, including engineers, economists and psychologists helped Federal agencies develop efficient, well-regulated procedures and plans. These ideas remain influential today, with business, industry and education believing in the inevitable logic of ever-increasing efficiency and productivity. Like other states during the Bush and Clinton years, Texas introduced reforms that emphasised control, uniformity and output. Teachers were forced to teach watered down content simply because it was computer gradable. Tests generated convenient data that could be used to judge schools and teachers (McNeil, 2000).

Talk of efficiency was alien to the education service in the UK before the 1988 Reform Act. Schools were virtually untouched by the management knowledge that had developed in industry, commerce and the armed forces. An alternative, patriarchal conception of educational leadership prevailed. The headmaster tradition was permeated with personal, moral and cultural concerns (Grace, 1995). The localised, differentiated structure of education was also unresponsive to managerial influences. Grammar, technical and secondary modern schools were subject to different expectations and followed separate paths. Examination results were not the universal preoccupation they have since become. Unscientific and unmanaged, this regime and philosophy persisted until the 1980s. Local authorities often assumed that all schools were making reasonable progress, so little was done to identify, remove or improve poor quality teaching (Dennison, 1998).

Effectiveness and improvement

This local, unsystematic approach was also encouraged and protected by the widespread belief that student achievement was closely linked to social conditions. Jackson and Marsden (1962) assembled evidence of the extent to which the middle-class was favoured by the tripartite school system in the UK. The previously strong confidence in the US that rational, scientific systems would produce good results for everyone was sharply reduced by reports that social and economic variables were decisive for student performance.

Schools were increasingly seen as agents of cultural reproduction, part of a matrix of social processes that resisted change and restricted mobility (Bernstein, 1977). Education was not expected to break the cycle of wealth and disadvantage and the characteristics of a school's intake were believed to determine outcomes (Jencks et al, 1972). The perceived performance of the early comprehensives in the UK and the apparent failure of Federal interventions in the US seemed to confirm the extent to which social reality compromised the potential of any non-selective school.

The seminal study *Fifteen Thousand Hours* (Rutter et al, 1979) challenged this pessimism and many of the assumptions on which previous policies had been based. Twelve London secondary schools in similar, unfavourable environments were shown to achieve very different results. Once a suitable adjustment was made for variations in the background and ability of the children attending each school, intake no longer seemed to be the factor that determined results. Observation revealed that in lessons where pupils were actively engaged the outcomes were better. *Fifteen Thousand*

Hours encouraged academics and policy-makers to become interested in the variables that influence school performance and to be less concerned with social conditions.

The discovery of hard, empirical evidence that schools and teachers could make a difference proved liberating and stimulated research into school effectiveness and improvement, with education policy and research in the US and UK moving in a broadly similar direction. What school-based factors were associated with success? The main features of school effectiveness research at that time included:

- a primary focus on student outcomes
- the study of formal organisation rather than informal processes or cultures
- a concern with the characteristics of schools already deemed to be effective
- a static methodology producing cross-sectional or snap shot pictures of the variables studied. (Gray *et al*, 1999)

The picture that emerged was remarkably consistent. Wilson and Corcoran (1988) identified nine structural dimensions associated with effectiveness, while Sammons *et al* (1995) tabulate eleven very similar factors found consistently in a wide range of studies, even when these were completed in apparently dissimilar education systems. Effective leaders ensure a shared vision, high expectations, clarity and fairness. Professional development is emphasised; pupils have rights and responsibilities. Effective schools are more tightly organised than less effective ones and operate as an organic whole rather than as a miscellaneous collection of departments. A large number of studies conclude that while school and classroom effects are not exceptionally large, they are educationally and statistically significant. By the 1980s, school and classroom factors were believed to account for up to eighteen per cent of the variance in pupils' achievement (Creemers, 1994). This margin contrasts sharply with the orthodoxy established in the 1960s and helps explain why the search for factors associated with effectiveness became so attractive. The effectiveness tradition drew strength from its attack on sociological pessimism.

Disappointed with centrally-led curriculum reform during the 1960s and 1970s, improvement researchers were equally encouraged by this new emphasis on internal school processes. Teachers and school culture had been ignored in the rush to introduce innovative schemes and methods. Fullan (1982, p84) concluded:

> It is easier to put a person on the moon than to attain the goal of raising reading levels across the country, because the factors keeping reading at its current level are innumerable, different in different situations, constantly changing, and not conducive to altering on any wide scale.

The advocates of change had failed to understand that the culture of complex, traditional organisations could not be modified quickly and that innovative plans had to allow space and time for those involved. The solution, it seemed, was to initiate and implement change at school level, shifting control as close as possible to the action (Hopkins, 1984). School improvement, it was now believed, should be owned by the school, not imposed from outside. An organisation's capacity for development and growth should be built over time by working on internal conditions to achieve cultural change (Harris, 2001).

During the 1980s, school improvement became a global concern, with the International School Improvement Project (ISIP) launched in 1982 at Palm Beach in the US drawing together 40 institutions from fourteen countries to consider a wide range of approaches, methods and case studies (Van Velzen, 1987). ISIP emphasised the school as the prime unit of change and gave careful attention to the qualitative factors that comprised the internal conditions of the school.

In the UK forty volunteer schools in East Anglia, North London and Yorkshire joined in partnership with the Cambridge Institute to form the Improving the Quality of Education for All (IQEA) project. IQEA adopted an empowering approach, with tutors challenging teachers to increase their capacity to handle change. Authority and hierarchy were seen as obstacles to improvement, so the tutors stressed active collaboration rather than leadership. The concept of effectiveness seemed to explain the divergence between the best performing schools and the rest, while improvement initiatives suggested that the gap could be closed. The hunt was on for methods that worked and made a difference.

The 1988 Education Act reinforced the attention given to the characteristics and performance of individual schools and so ensured the continued, pervasive influence of the effectiveness paradigm. LMS and GMS schools were made directly accountable for their own efficiency and results. Parental choice, pupil-based funding and published information, including examination results and inspection reports, were designed to create an education market place where schools would sink or swim in the pursuit of pupils and budgets. Accountability and competition were supposed to stimulate teachers to improve effectiveness, add value and increase productivity (Grace, 1995, Davies and Hentschke, 1998). Effective schools with good results would attract increased numbers and larger budgets; less successful schools would wither on the vine.

The concept of effectiveness provided a circular justification for reform, with test and examination results used to define and measure student achievement and to validate the characteristics of successful schools. When Ofsted was established in 1992, the new inspection criteria were closely aligned with the effectiveness characteristics identified by Sammons *et al* (1995). Schools were expected to comply with organisational practices associated with effectiveness and to achieve annual increments in their results (Fitz *et al*, 2000).

Margin of improvement

Although the effectiveness paradigm remains the corner-stone of government policy, enabling schools to be measured and judged, the theoretical and technical weaknesses of the underlying concepts have become increasingly evident. Despite their shared concern with individual schools, the improvement and effectiveness traditions are almost critiques of one another (Fidler, 2001). Improvers work with the intangibles of cultural change but are reluctant to assess student outcomes; while effectiveness experts measure the correlation between characteristics and results but are unable to explain how schools become effective over time. The improvement approach is concerned with collegiality, empowerment and shared values and says little about heads or leadership; effectiveness research reports that 'professional leadership' is an essential feature of successful schools.

Effectiveness research is also widely criticised for choosing variables that fail to capture the organisational complexity they seek to describe and for interpreting correlations between factors as evidence of causal mechanisms. When the selected factors are not distinct from one another in nature, making them discrete conceptually can distort our understanding of what is taking place (Carspecken, 1996). Variables interact with one another in complex ways so that apparently similar circumstances do not produce identical results.

In the changed policy climate brought about by the election of a New Labour government in 1997, there is renewed doubt about whether effective schools really can overcome poverty. Disadvantage seems to have cumulative effects for poor children who are physically weaker than their peers and more vulnerable to emotional tensions in their lives. The strongly negative correlation between measures of social disadvantage and school achievement persists. A small number of schools may disturb the 'long term patterning of educational inequality' but the likelihood of their challenge being sustained over time is small (Mortimore and Whitty, 2000, p10).

Advanced statistical techniques have enabled large data sets to be analysed, with results that have reduced the performance margin believed to be influenced by school factors. Gray *et al* (1995) estimate that between-school variance is no more than five per cent in models that incorporate prior attainment measures and indicate that the proportion of pupils from professional homes is an important predictor of examination results. In Sheffield, up to 95 per cent of the difference in results can be explained by poverty, gender and attendance (Davies, 2000). Studies like these have led to speculation that the balance or social mix of a school's intake may be the single most important influence on variations in student performance (Thrupp, 1999). Local school hierarchies seem to shape and compound differences between schools:

> Schools low down the hierarchy, which are therefore characterised by a high concentration of socially disadvantaged students relative to other schools, have particular difficulties in improving academic results. (Levačić and Woods, 2002a, p222)

Disadvantage, mediated by intricate social mixing mechanisms within and between local communities, may produce many of the phenomena currently attributed to variations in school characteristics. Government ministers and officials are reluctant to admit that, after several decades, reform has made little impression on educational inequality, while the margin available for influence by institutional variables may be rather small. The effectiveness paradigm seems to be in trouble.

Accountability and turbulence

After 1988, policy-makers in the UK emphasised 'market-shaped entrepreneurship' (Grace, 1995, p23) rather than leadership to improve the quality of education. Secondary headteachers began to behave like chief executives, devoting their time and energy to budgets, management systems and public relations rather than teaching and classrooms. Although instructional leadership was recognised as an important feature of effective schools, for most heads the priority was to manage the turbulence unleashed by the 1988 Education Act. Bell (1988), writing before the legislation was enacted, describes an unpredictable, unstable environment where school leaders struggled to make sense of a multiplicity of changes. The Secretary of State, Kenneth Baker, expected the new, market-led system to disrupt traditional practices and release latent creative energy but very often the chaos and flux following the 1988 legislation distracted attention from the classroom (Ribbins and Sherratt, 1997, Cutler, 1991). Heads were more concerned with managing government initiatives than with leading their own initiatives. The School Management Task Force (1990) recommended 'visionary leadership' but failed to develop a persuasive picture of how leaders should impact on the quality of teaching and learning.

Almost by default, accountability and standards became the enduring policy theme of the 1990s (Fullan, 2003). In the UK, governments showed surprisingly little interest in helping schools to improve their leadership and raise their game. Instead, the regulatory regime was tightened. The Office of Her Majesty's Chief Inspector was established by the 1992 Education Act, with the aim of increasing the pressure on schools to learn the lessons of effectiveness research and to improve results. The new inspection office, known as Ofsted, penetrated every nook and cranny of the school system. Commencing in September 1993, Ofsted inspected all 24,000 schools at least once and many of them up to three times (Fitz *et al*, 2000). Published reports comment on standards in relation to national norms and identify strengths and weaknesses in a school's effectiveness.

The inspection system was widely regarded as:

> A form of regulation by the market to encourage higher standards in schools ... the clear objective of the publication of league tables and so on is to use a kind of market mechanism to improve standards in schools. (House of Commons, 1999a, px)

Governors are required within 40 days of the publication of the inspection report to produce an action plan and this is regarded as an essential tool for school improvement. Ofsted (1994, p3) advises that:

> Action plans are primarily concerned with raising achievement ... and incorporate: specific targets for raising standards ... practical strategies ... focus on these goals; and arrangements for monitoring and evaluating the progress.

Ofsted's improvement strategy is controversial, however, and has aroused strongly negative emotions amongst many teachers. Critics question whether inspection can bring about improvement. Schools are bound to take notice of Ofsted criteria and to respond to inspection judgements but it is more doubtful whether the process can arouse sustained commitment. There are few studies of the effects of inspection on subsequent progress and little evidence that inspection produces tangible benefits. A study of six schools in five LEAs found that twelve months after inspection only seven out of 43 recommendations made by inspectors had been implemented, and that after eighteen months only seventeen had been fully adopted. The researchers detected no serious attempt by the heads involved to base long term strategies on inspection recommendations and argue that superficial compliance is the most likely outcome of the process. There is only limited evidence that children's learning has improved as a result of action plan targets. Inspection privileges the voice of the inspectors but may not motivate those who have to take the required action (Gray and Wilcox, 1995).

Fitz *et al* (2000) claim that the purpose of Ofsted inspections is:

> ...to secure some homogeneity of curriculum, pedagogical and assessment practice, management procedures and efficiency in an education system ... previously characterised by large variation in all these areas.

Unfortunately there is little evidence that increased homogeneity and consistency alone can improve a school's effectiveness.

Fear of failure

Ofsted's power to declare that schools are failing or have serious weaknesses has an impact across the system that is dispropor-tionate to the numbers directly affected. Governors, heads and teachers are fearful of being placed in special measures and are therefore more likely to comply with national policies and initiatives. The threat of punishment concentrates minds and prompts obedience. Consequently Ofsted has been in a strong posi-tion to influence choices and priorities. Sustained pressure has been applied to ensure that schools adopt scientific planning pro-cedures, monitor student achievement and use performance data to inform development.

There is limited evidence that this pressure has produced improve-ment. Few of the two per cent of secondary schools actually placed in special measures achieve a long term improvement in GCSE results (Fitz *et al*, 2000). Academic results often slip backwards after inspection (House of Commons, 1999b). The Office for Standards in Inspection (1999) concludes that:

> ...the system discourages schools and teachers from thinking for themselves; instead it encourages them to become dependent on instructions from Ofsted ... as a result, teachers are in danger of losing the confidence and professionalism which makes for excit-ing schools and good teaching.

The inspection regime has clarified public expectations and has concentrated attention on standards and performance. Sadly, Ofsted's coercive methods can also damage morale and reduce initiative. By 1997, when New Labour came to power, policy-makers were ready to recognise the need for support as well as pressure and to listen to evidence from the US that positive leadership can raise motivation and commitment (Litwin and Stringer, 1968).

A new paradigm

As American business faced the economic crisis of the seventies and eighties, the limitations of large hierarchical organisations and scientific management were exposed. The stable conditions of large-scale mass production had ceased to exist and firms had to adapt to changes in the environment if they were to survive. Falling profits prompted a search for new solutions. Academics from business schools studied the features of the best run companies and discovered that strong leaders played an important part in the pursuit of excellence. According to Peters and Waterman (1995) successful companies:

- had a bias for action
- were close to the customer
- fostered leadership through the organisation
- achieved productivity through people
- were driven by values
- were focused on their core business
- adopted a flat, simple structure
- and were simultaneously tight around core values and loose in being flexible and responsive.

The conclusion was that leaders could be a decisive influence on their organisations, especially by raising their employees' motivation and performance:

> ...leaders can expect to transform their organisations and their people by communicating vision, clarifying purposes, making behaviour congruent with belief, and aligning procedures with principles, roles and goals. (Covey, 1992, p69)

Although these ideas of transformation and empowerment came from American business, they were not really compatible with the 'chief executive' model of leadership encouraged by the Conservative reforms (Chitty, 1989). New Labour found transformational leadership a much more congenial theme.

The new government's early insistence on effectiveness and standards was accompanied by a new prominence for leadership and active policies to improve its quality. *Excellence in Schools* (Department for Education and Employment, 1997) insisted that good heads could transform their schools and that all new and serving heads should be trained to match the performance of the best. In 2000 the Secretary of State announced the launch of the NCSL as a new partner in the drive to raise standards. The college would:

> ...play a key role in the Government's strategy to transform our schools, drive up standards and ensure that every school is excellent or improving or both. (Blunkett, 2000, p1)

Labour also drew on the school improvement tradition, with its growing emphasis on internal capacity and culture. Fullan (2000b) claims that a leader's main role is to develop the capacity for reform whilst the IQEA partnership has generated evidence that leadership is a vital factor in bringing about change (West *et al*, 2000). This transformational paradigm has replaced the chief executive model that emerged in the 1990s and informs the *National Standards* (Teacher Training Agency, 2001). Heads are expected to 'lead by example, provide inspiration and motivation' and 'embody the vision, purpose and leadership of the school'.

The growing confidence that transformational leaders can achieve dramatic improvements, even in the most unpromising, disadvantaged circumstances, is reinforced by the example of schools that have been turned round (Clark, 1998). Fullan (2000a) now believes that 'schools can be taken out of special measures status in about nineteen to 22 months by employing strong intervention methods.' The long nurtured assumptions of the school improvement movement were aligned at last with the convictions of mainstream educators and politicians.

Transformational leadership

Since 2001 the NCSL has advocated a model of leadership based mainly on research in the US and has developed a range of programmes to facilitate school transformation, including the Leadership Programme for Serving Headteachers (LPSH), the National Professional Qualification for Headship (NPQH) and Leading from the Middle. School leaders are enjoined to learn and adopt leadership styles and habits that should facilitate capacity and culture building, improve motivation, empower colleagues and enhance performance (NCSL, 2003). Litwin and Stringer (1968), Burns (1978) and McClelland (1987) have been particularly influential in shaping the idea that leaders can mobilise a range of resources to motivate followers and raise them to higher levels of commitment and achievement.

Burns hoped to base a general theory of leadership on an historical analysis of great leaders and their effects. His transformational model was intended to provide an inclusive alternative to the top down managerialism that dominated US business at the time. Burns distinguishes between *transactional* leaders who secure a series of deals to achieve their goals and *transforming* leaders who raise followers to a higher moral level in pursuit of their idealistic vision. Transactional leaders engage in an extended bargaining process with subordinates whose private interests may come before the needs of the organisation. Transformational leaders, by contrast, work by stages to convert people's self-centred, conflicting values and goals into an altruistic concern for a collective moral enterprise.

Consultants and researchers have been attracted by the idea of a leader who can engage followers in a moral endeavour that transforms unproductive and even destructive patterns of behaviour. Peters and Waterman (1995) emphasise the need for transforming business leaders to create a culture of excellence; Caldwell and Spinks (1992) recognise that transformational leadership is equally relevant in the setting of the self-managing school. Bass and Avolio (1994) explain how leaders can use idealised influence, inspirational motivation, intellectual stimulation and individualised consideration to raise followers to higher levels. Transformational leaders should not use power for personal gain and must be role models for their followers, who identify with them and seek to emulate their behaviour. Leaders should provide meaning and challenge so that subordinates are inspired and motivated to pursue a shared vision. They should also listen carefully as they acknowledge each individual's need for achievement and growth and delegate responsibility as a means of developing potential.

The transformational model has been tested empirically in a number of school settings. An American case study reports how a high school principal created an empowering culture. Mary Doe brought about remarkable improvements as she worked through the transactional, transitional and transformational stages of leadership (Starratt, 1999). Another investigation in the US measured leadership behaviour on two spectra, from transactional to transformative and from closed to open. When school principals chose open styles and were less concerned to control their colleagues, the quality of relationships was transformed. 71 per cent of teacher participants reported negative outcomes for their classroom and school wide performance when principals adopted closed, transactional styles. Open, transformative principals were perceived to be far more effective and to have a positive effect on teachers (Blase and Anderson, 1995).

Work at 83 schools in Ontario suggests that leaders can invite their colleagues to join them in creating a shared and evolving vision and in bringing about the conditions and cultural norms that are conducive to improvement (Stoll and Fink, 1995). A similar phenomenon has been noted in the UK. At twelve schools:

> ...enormous amounts of time and energy were invested in building the kinds of collaborative cultures inside and outside the school which were consistent with the heads' values and visions... (Day *et al*, 2000, p58)

The heads were seen to develop a post-transformational, values-led contingency form of leadership that aimed to reconcile competing beliefs and interests and to create the climate for sustained improvement.

Sergiovanni (1995) identifies four sources of authority for the new, powerful but also empowering version of leadership envisaged by much of the literature. He concludes that heads should draw on:

- bureaucratic authority, with an emphasis on rules, mandates and regulations, in an effort to direct thought and action
- interpersonal style and political guile to achieve thought and action
- professional authority based on knowledge of best practice
- moral authority that asks people to respond by doing their duty.

Accumulating authority by these means, heads should then barter, build, bond and bind, according to the stage they have reached.

These ambitious theories of transformation are underpinned by research into the relationship between leadership and motivation. McClelland and Burnham (1995) observe that the best managers are interested in using socialised power to benefit the organisation as a whole and are not concerned to be liked by people. These leaders are emotionally mature and adopt democratic and coaching styles. They create workplace climates that empower subordinates and arouse positive motivation. Authoritarian, bullying behaviour has the opposite effect, stimulating compliance and submission.

Litwin and Stringer (1968) explore the impact of leadership behaviour on organisational climate and motivation. The presidents of three simulated business organisations each adopted a distinctive style, intended to arouse one of three social motives.

- Organisation A was led to arouse the need for power, defined as the need to control or influence others and to control the means of influencing others. The director insisted on rules, control, order, standards and criticism of poor performance.

- Organisation B was directed to arouse the need for affiliation, defined as the need for close interpersonal relationships and friendships with other people. The director encouraged informality, positive rewards, a relaxed atmosphere, cooperation and warm personal relationships.

- Organisation C aimed to arouse the need for achievement, defined as the need for success in relation to an internalised standard of excellence. The director stressed informality, high standards for individuals and the organisation, rewards for excellent performance, cooperation, stress and challenge.

The climate produced by these styles was measured by asking employees to rate their perceptions of how they were treated on six dimensions. These were:

- How much compliance with rules is expected
- The amount of responsibility given
- The emphasis on quality and standards

- How far rewards exceed criticism for mistakes
- How clear are goals and objectives
- How warm and supportive the organisation feels, and the extent to which team spirit is fostered.

After two weeks, it was apparent that leadership styles could produce distinct organisational climates:

> Such climates can be created in a short period of time, and their characteristics are quite stable ... Once created, these climates seem to have significant ... effects on motivation, and correspondingly on performance and job satisfaction. (p144)

Organisation C proved easily the most successful.

Leaders who learn to manage their own motives and select an appropriate combination of styles should be able to create an achievement-oriented organisational climate which will enhance performance and productivity. The experiment has provided persuasive evidence for the claim that leaders can transform the behaviour of their subordinates and has informed a variety of training programmes that claim to enhance leadership capacity.

Leadership development

The leadership programme (LPSH) adopted by the NCSL is based on Hay Group's research into headteacher characteristics as well as these conclusions about the relationship between styles, climate and motivation. Consultants conducted structured interviews with 121 heads and deputies to identify and define the characteristics associated with success. Hay found fifteen characteristics that distinguish 'highly effective' headteachers from the rest. Heads who demonstrate the capacity for 'developing potential', 'holding people accountable' and 'transformational leadership' are believed to deliver exceptional school performance (NCSL, 2003).

LPSH believes that headteachers' personal characteristics prompt them to adopt particular combinations of leadership styles that may impact on school climate, and consequently on teacher and student motivation. Climate is measured on six dimensions, similar to those used in the Litwin and Stringer experiment. In advance of the programme, the participants and five selected colleagues complete questionnaires on their perceptions of the qualities displayed by the head and of the climate produced at the school. Characteristics, styles and climate dimensions are defined in systematic, consistent language that participants have found useful (Collarbone, 2001). Hay Diagnostics analyse the questionnaires, norm-reference the data and provide feedback to help participants plan for improvement.

Using coercive and pace-setting styles inappropriately has been found to reduce the extent to which employees feel responsible and committed, while authoritative and coaching styles are said to have a positive, motivating influence (NCSL, 2003). Barker (2001) examined data on six case study headteachers to test the usefulness of the LPSH model. More successful heads were reported to use the authoritative and coaching styles, whilst the 'poor performers' adopted the coercive, pace-setting styles said to produce low morale and weak performance.

Heads are encouraged to select the right permutation of styles for the situation encountered. The programme claims that as leadership is responsible for 70 per cent of the climate, heads who optimise their choice of styles, through training, reflection and practice, can secure large, potentially transforming improvements in motivation and commitment.

Improving performance

For the NCSL, transformational leadership is unproblematic. LPSH programme participants are encouraged to believe that they are developing the ability to bring about remarkable improvements in performance. Enthusiasts are convinced that school leaders are vital agents of social change and argue that:

> ...the moral imperative of the principal involves leading deep cultural change that mobilises the passion and commitment of teachers, parents, and others to improve the learning of all students, including closing the achievement gap... (Fullan, 2003, p41)

As we have seen, this optimistic view disregards evidence that social influences limit what can be achieved. There is little empirical data to support the claim that leaders can close the achievement gap or motivate teachers to improve their lessons to the point where value-added performance is significantly enhanced. No direct link has been established between leadership and results:

Hallinger and Heck discovered that the common professional and public assumption of large principal leadership effects on school outcomes, an assumption accounting for the key role assumed by school reform initiatives, was not warranted. Instead, their analyses suggested that principal effects were small and usually required exceptionally sophisticated research designs to detect. (Leithwood and Jantzi, 2000, p50)

There are few in-depth studies of how schools develop and change over time (Fink, 1999) and there is no evidence that transformational leadership on its own can produce anything but 'modest improved consequences for pupil outcomes' (Gold *et al*, 2003, p129). Pre-existing differences in performance between schools are much more important than *changes* in their effectiveness (Gray *et al*, 1999); and as yet there are no clear links between improved student outcomes and collaborative, democratic and distributed forms of leadership (Harris, 2004).

This is hardly surprising, given how difficult it is to measure leadership impact on school performance. A head's behaviour is not an independent variable producing predictable and distinctive effects. Rather, leaders are part of a complex interaction of people and circumstances that are subject to a wide variety of influences. Individual leaders may struggle to sustain a consistent, positive repertoire of styles through the disparate stages of life and headship; and may find it equally difficult to maintain collaborative relationships with senior colleagues over a prolonged period. An uncharted, unexplored succession of leaders at different levels may have contributed to a particular outcome or set of results. School improvement is a long term enterprise and inevitably includes an immense number of intricate, multi-faceted relationships and variables that are not easy to disentangle.

Style and motivation

The LPSH style descriptors chosen to measure heads' behaviour are internally consistent and enable participants to be compared. Unfortunately the everyday language used to define each style is value laden and compromises the validity and reliability of the methodology. An expression like 'Relies on negative, corrective feedback' (NCSL, 2003), for example, may imply disapproval of the coercive style. Heads are inclined to describe their own styles in terms with positive associations, such as open or consultative, in preference to those with negative connotations like closed and autocratic. The analysis of styles can collapse into 'an endless typology of forms' (Grace, 1995, p37) while labels like 'coercive' and 'democratic' may exclude as much as they explain. Attempts to analyse behaviour in terms of a combination of styles are likely to be unsatisfactory because the mixture can become so complex that the link with the original criteria is lost or tenuous (Evans, 1999, p30).

The feminist perspective also challenges the assumptions and language used to describe and explain leadership. Stereotypically masculine qualities are said to dominate the literature, producing a biased impression of leadership that excludes women. Authoritarian, charismatic, entrepreneurial and competitive behaviour seem to be particularly associated with males. Female leaders are reported to adopt different, less aggressive styles:

> Women's leadership style is less hierarchical and more democratic. Women, for example, run more closely knit schools than do men, and communicate better with teachers. They use different, less dominating, body language and different language and procedures. Women appear more flexible and sensitive and often more successful. (Ozga, 1993, p11)

Bem (1974) contrasts the analytical, assertive behaviour associated with males with female traits like affection and sympathy. Shakeshaft (1998) identifies significant differences in the way men and women manage. Women are said to:

- conduct more unscheduled meetings
- observe teachers more often
- have shorter desk sessions during the day
- interact more frequently with teachers, parents and women
- have more flexible agendas for meetings
- give more attention to individual differences between students
- see the job in educational rather than administrative terms.

The validity of these observations of workplace behaviour remains open to question. Twelve dissertations on sex differences found no divergence between males and females (Shakeshaft, 1998). The evidence on gender-based differences in style seems to be unreliable. Most of the studies have been American, small-scale and inconclusive (Evetts, 1994). We cannot be sure that masculine and feminine styles have an objective existence beyond the language used to describe them. Tannen (1996), for example, analyses gender differences in workplace conversation but is careful to acknowledge that there is nothing inherently male or female about particular ways of talking at work. Her data suggests only that more women than men are likely to put themselves at a disadvantage in competitive talking environments such as business meetings.

Gender stereotypes may in reality disguise more than they explain:

> There would seem to be little merit, then, in claiming that there are gender-derived styles, when in actual fact the leader style differences within gender categories ... are likely to be at least, or more, significant than those thought to exist between categories. (Gronn, 1999, p124)

We do not know whether men and women draw upon different repertoires or whether their choices are based on perceptions of gender-appropriate behaviour (Hall, 1998). The debate about whether leadership is 'different' for women illustrates, therefore, the limitations of the everyday language used to describe behaviour. Our discussion of leadership is inevitably permeated with hidden assumptions about values and social action.

The absence of consistent, stable definitions across a range of studies for styles variously labelled as charismatic, authoritarian or democratic calls into question whether they are real phenomena or generalisations without scientific foundation. For example, Ball's interpersonal, managerial, adversarial and authoritarian styles, described as ways of 'doing leadership within the everyday social reality of the school' (1987, p85) do not include the possibility of Blase and Anderson's (1995) shift from the authoritarian or adversarial to the facilitative and democratic. Although both studies use the language of micro-politics, their conceptions of leadership and style are quite different.

Headteacher effects cannot be measured reliably if the descriptors applied to styles and climate are ambiguous and open to interpretation. Leadership styles vary greatly but there is scant evidence that any particular style is associated with better outcomes for students (Rutter *et al*, 1979). It may be significant that the NCSL has chosen not to analyse performance trends at schools led by programme participants.

The NCSL claims that motivation is the key link between school leaders and teacher and student performance. Appropriate styles are said to increase discretionary effort and output. Although there are undoubtedly schools with low morale and disaffected staff it is less certain whether low levels of motivation are a widespread problem. The opposite may be the case, with high levels of professionalism leading to exhausted teachers. Calder (1969, pp117/118), writing in another context, warns against relying too heavily on the increased motivation and commitment of a workforce that is already overstretched. In 1940:

> ...all the workmen and supervision staff involved in radar at the Metropolitan Vickers factory in Manchester worked for forty-eight hours without a break to dispatch eight special transmitters ... (but) the new effort negated itself. Production rose by a quarter in the first week after Dunkirk; but by the fifth week it was practically the same as before, although sixty to seventy hours a week were still commonly worked ... Excessive hours produced fatigue and poor health, and so increased both voluntary and involuntary absence from work.

Blackmore (1993) suggests that post-modern organisations are greedy and exploitative and use the intimacy of personal relationships to stimulate motivation. Like any other manager, the transforming leader is mainly concerned to control the aim and purpose of the organisation and to maximise employee commitment by all available means. She believes that modern leadership theories have simply incorporated convenient ideas and rhetoric from democratic and feminist sources.

Leadership programmes that aim to improve quality and performance may also be frustrated in the longer term by heads who find it more difficult than expected to achieve the level of enduring personal change required to achieve a better style. Leaders are more likely than most to develop a compelling theory of action that guides behaviour and resists alternatives (Argyris, 1991). Mature thoughts and agendas are not easily altered. This helps explain why heads and principals often disparage university-style management training courses and even look for evidence to prove that theories have little practical value (Wolcott, 1984, Pitner, 1987).

Alternative visions

This instinctive resistance to neatly packaged scientific theories may be justified. The LPSH model is surprisingly one dimensional and draws on psychological experiment and questionnaires rather than the detailed observation of heads and senior teams leading improvement. Heads are acutely aware of the contextual complications that make it so hard to transfer prescribed methods and formulae from one setting to another (Hargreaves and Fink, 2001) and are naturally wary about acting on over-simple accounts of school life that lead us:

> ...to think in the rationalistic tradition about our work ... and to over-estimate the tightness of links between research and practice. (Sergiovanni, 1995, pix)

Almost forgotten ethnographic studies (Ball, 1981, Burgess, 1983, Wolcott, 1984) describe a world that is not easily explained in transformational terms. Schools like Beachside and Bishop McGregor are populated by teachers whose competing values and interests are unlikely to be transcended by someone else's superior moral vision. Confrontations and interaction between diverse individuals and groups produce a changing pattern of control rather than agreement about goals and objectives. Conflict can result in relatively low levels of coordination and integration, while the intentions and actions of the staff may be so loosely coupled that plans do not turn out as leaders expect (Weick, 1988).

Daily life appears very different from the rational processes described in most textbooks. Managers plan on the hoof and prefer gossip, hearsay and speculation to the data produced by their elaborate management information systems (Mintzberg, 1975). Ofsted-style action plans and targets seem strangely at odds with the human reality of offices and classrooms. Competing interests produce messy decisions and unintended consequences, while ceaseless pressures distract managers from their formal administrative responsibilities. One principal told Wolcott (1984, p229):

> ...just keeping the school functioning is almost more than one person can handle ... I don't spend 25 per cent of my time with the people who are handling the instructional program.

Hall *et al* (1986, p205) were surprised by the extent to which heads seem to be driven by events and neglect wider strategic considerations. Observers reported:

> ...their daily work to be fragmented, people-intensive and to encompass a range of tasks. Teaching emerged as the longest sustained activity for many headteachers and formal scheduled meetings constituted a low proportion of the job.

School leaders were found to spend their time in brief, fragmented encounters and to operate in a micro-political milieu that drives priorities. Strategies and plans seemed less pressing than the immediate demands of their colleagues and students. Aware of this reality, Wolcott (1984) interprets the relationship between the principal and the school in essentially conservative terms. The task of the school leader is to attend to those factors that promote stability and to manage and contain the forces of change when these appear to threaten organisational continuity and survival.

The messy particulars of these ethnographic descriptions are not easily captured in a single conceptual framework. The unpredictable interactions of human agency and structure continue to produce discomfiting data that prompts the adaptation and elaboration of successive models of leadership. Transformational leaders are now encouraged to be invitational, instructional and distributive because heroic leadership alone seems to have made little difference to the examination results. Attempts to transcend the swampy difficulties of school life also prompt dissent. Gronn (1998), for example, claims that human agency has been exaggerated. People are culturally conditioned to attribute their successes and failures to a leader or manager who symbolises or personifies their organisation. Astuto and Clark (1986) believe that leaders are effectively empowered by followers whose actions and words define the scope of what is possible. According to Allix (2000) transformational leadership could create the conditions for dictatorship. How do followers successfully question the values and goals proposed by a charismatic leader?

Such disputes about leadership seem inevitable because the field of:

> ...educational administration is neither unitary nor homogeneous nor monolithic. It is fragmented and factional, obscure in its dimensions, vague in its ends, and contentious in its methodologies. (Hodgkinson, 1993, px)

Disagreements about leadership and reform have also produced internal tensions within and between government agencies. Advocates of transformational leadership, like the NCSL, dwell on visions and values but their humane, moral approach has to work within a structure of bureaucratic accountability that measures only efficiency and effectiveness (MacIntyre, 1993). Heads may have visions so long as they lead to an increase in test results. The same government has promoted and encouraged Ofsted and LPSH, despite their contrasting thoughts about human motivation. The effectiveness and improvement traditions represent distinctive approaches to researching and understanding schools that are not easily reconciled.

Even the criteria used to measure the quality and effectiveness of education are in dispute:

> The terms of 'good' and 'effective' are not neutral but contested. The notion of a good school is a social construct, shaped by national expectations and local aspirations ... the notion of an effective school is socially constructed. (Riley and MacBeath, 1998, p143)

Standardised tests prevail although they narrow the curriculum, exclude the personal knowledge that teachers and students bring to the classroom and reward test sophistication rather than creativity. Teachers are expected to limit themselves to a narrow range of techniques for improving results in areas where straightforward answers are available (Angus, 2002).

These confused debates stem from modern uncertainties about authority, values and language, a resulting difference in the interpretation of social organisations and sustained disagreement about the nature of scientific method and the validity of different types of evidence (Kuhn, 1975). The problem is that:

> The twentieth century has seen a disintegration of conventional
> and traditional authority and morality and we have not yet for-
> mulated the possibilities of a new order. (West, 1991, p26)

The contemporary emphasis on science and bureaucracy and our
reliance on experts (Giddens, 1991) is a predictable reaction to lost
certainties and the danger of subjectivism. The fact that the
National Curriculum was constructed without reference to an overarching framework is an example of how bureaucratic processes
can exclude values in favour of appeals to rationality and efficiency
(White, 1987).

Ethical and moral issues are inescapable in schools, however, and
present themselves through a continuous multiplicity of tensions
and dilemmas:

> ...competing value orientations manifest themselves ... Adminis-
> trators become aware of values issues without any particular need
> for prior training in philosophy, or exposure to the literature on
> administrative ethics. (Begley, 1999, p52)

Government agencies are bureaucracies, created to ensure that
schools are rational, scientifically managed institutions, while
heads and teachers have to deal with the unresolved dilemmas
generated by modern, pluralist societies (Kruchov *et al*, 1998). NCSL
programmes do not encourage reflection on moral dilemmas or
conflicts between values. West grumbles that 'any value-conflicts
which might arise from the absence of legitimated macro aims are
left to the schools and their stakeholders to work out' (1993, p24).
Leadership seems to be a moral art rather than a science of improvement, requiring wisdom and judgement to manage values,
resolve conflicts and determine priorities (Hodgkinson, 1991).

Critical perspectives like these challenge the scientific theories that
are supposed to explain human organisations. School leadership
has become an 'arena of struggle' (Gunter, 2001) where hopes of
'closing the achievement gap' (Fullan, 2003) may be lost in a ceaseless debate about value and meaning. The theories and conceptual
frameworks described in this chapter provide, therefore, diverse
viewpoints from which to interpret events at Hillside, each with distinctive priorities and assumptions about the nature of change.
These include:

Primary Concern	**Source of Change**
■ Efficiency and effectiveness	Scientific management; rational plans
■ Improving internal conditions	Staff ownership and participation
■ Accountability and inspection	Pressure to comply with prescribed standards
■ Leadership styles, behaviour	Shared vision; staff motivation
■ Conflicting values and goals	Struggle
■ Tension and conflict between internal processes and external demands	Situational contingencies
■ Socio-economic conditions in the local environment	Intake composition; variations in the mix or balance of student admissions

These discordant voices suggest the questions that should be asked about how leaders influence their schools and help define the areas where case study evidence can assist our understanding of change and improvement:

■ Can leaders calculate their behaviour to improve motivation and moral commitment?

■ To what extent are leaders constrained by contextual, cultural and micro-political variables that impact on change?

■ Is there a transferable set of best practice recommendations that can be adopted anywhere?

■ Can we hope to close the achievement gap, despite the known links between poverty and low achievement?

Chapters three to six describe Hillside's journey through special measures and provide detailed evidence for the discussion of these fundamental questions in chapter seven.

3

Sleeping Giant

School and community

Hillside is one of the twenty one schools that serve Easton, a vibrant, medium-sized university town. The visitor drives northwards from the city centre on an arterial road lined with tall Victorian terraces and inter-war semi-detached housing before bearing left into the leafy suburban avenues of Hillside, a relatively affluent area developed in the middle years of the twentieth century. The school's cluster of low-rise, pebble-dashed blocks is built into the contours that rise above the river Ease as it flows out from the town into the open rural landscape beyond.

The immediate neighbourhood of the school is affluent, with a 'strong bias towards the professional and managerial socio-economic groups' (Acorn profile). The proportion of the eleven plus entry coming from Hillside declined during the 1990s as the eleven plus student population in the area fell. More families were drawn from postcodes scattered across the northern half of the city, particularly from Brownville, a large council estate on the far side of the arterial road. Brownville is an older industrial area where the 'relatively poor health of many people gives rise to significant social problems' (Acorn profile). Student numbers were predicted to rise slightly in the late 1990s.

Easton LEA schools, including Hillside, lagged behind in the national school performance tables. On average only thirty five per cent achieved the magic five or more GCSE A* – C grades during the period of the study, making them vulnerable to the criticism that their students were under-achieving. Only twenty seven per cent of Hillside students obtained five or more higher grades at the time of the fatal Ofsted inspection. The head's form prepared for Ofsted confirms the mixed but relatively disadvantaged nature of the intake. Almost twenty per cent of students were on the SEN register, while twenty three per cent were eligible for free school meals. Of those on the register, almost twenty per cent were placed at stages three to five of the SEN Code of Practice because of various disabilities.

Over twenty per cent of the students came from homes where English was not the first language. Punjabi, Gujarati, French and Khachi were among the languages spoken. Approximately thirty per cent had non-English ethnic backgrounds, mainly Indian but also African, Caribbean and Chinese. Of the ten boys excluded in the previous year (five permanently, five fixed term), eight were white. The school's intake included more boys (54 per cent) than girls (46 per cent).

The main trends in the composition of the intake are clear. Hillside School attracted:

- a declining, predominantly white middle-class intake from the Hillside ward; an increasing, disadvantaged, predominantly white working-class intake from the southern part of the Brownville estate and elsewhere

- a growing number of relatively prosperous Indian families as they moved from the town centre to buy private property in the outer suburbs, especially to the south and west of Hillside.

Albert Wake at Hillside

Albert Wake had been in post for over twenty years when Ofsted arrived to inspect Hillside. He had opened the school in the 1970s and appointed many teachers who found the place comfortable and remained there for the rest of their professional lives. At the time of the inspection, eight members of staff had served over twenty years. The average full-time teacher had sixteen years experience and had worked at the school for ten of them. Only eight teachers had left during the previous two years.

The inspection judgement on Mr Wake's headship was uncompromising and came to overshadow other memories of those long years:

> Hillside School has a number of important weaknesses in standards of attainment, the quality of teaching and in its management and efficiency. Many of these weaknesses arise from serious shortcomings in the quality of leadership and management provided to the school by the headteacher and governing body.

Mr Wake claimed to have expected this outcome: 'I wasn't surprised, I never fitted, they collected data to prove I was at fault; staff were happy to blame me.' Elaine, a year head who later became deputy head and helped lead Hillside out of special measures, summed up her perceptions:

> On a personal level he could be ... rude, blunt, aggressive, all very negative ... but on another level, he could be actually quite pleasant, quite jovial, quite amenable, and actually quite considerate, particularly if you had personal circumstances that were more difficult at the time ... But on a professional level he could often be quite ignorant ... he was a bit of a Jekyll and Hyde figure and you were never quite sure which you were gonna get.

Darren, a young newly qualified teacher, reported a similar uncertainty about how Mr Wake might react: 'He taught my subject ... I found him a very nice bloke, personally ... you might say something and the reaction you would get ... would be quite negative.' Eleanor, a special needs teacher, said that: '...he was very good to me ... he was a very disillusioned person. He was very remote.' Anne, a long serving office assistant who eventually became personal assistant to the senior management team, remarked that he was 'a very pleasant man but I felt he glossed over things.' The caretaker felt that 'Mr Wake wasn't all that charming really ... he sometimes seems to look like he was in a bad mood so you don't feel confident' while Jean, head of year ten, saw him 'as an anonymous figure, never smiled, ignored people ... If you greeted him he would often ignore you. It was quite rude. It had an influence on the rest of the work of the school.' One year eleven student complained: 'I don't think anyone really liked Mr Wake. I think his method was too strict and it made the school feel gloomy and not really enthusiastic.'

Mr Wake considered himself to be 'an awkward sod, always have been, I go my own way, take no notice of them, I don't fit.' He admitted that: 'I don't suffer fools gladly' and expressed impatience with heads' meetings. At first he had attended but then 'it struck me it could all be written down on a side of A4'. As the head of an eleven to sixteen school, he was dismissive of middle schools where there was 'no conception of GCSE'. Like Eleanor, who said that 'he wasn't a traditional type of head ... he wasn't a man to give impressions', Mr Wake saw himself as a nonconformist who did not comply with official expectations. 'I was the track suited head,' he said, 'I didn't fit the model, I loved being with the children.' He agreed that he could be uncompromising with his colleagues but 'when people are down it's different, I'm hard but not when they can't take it.'

Mr Wake attributed many of his difficulties to the local authority. In his opinion the county had mismanaged the school from the start. He had never found out who advertised the first jobs at Hillside and claimed that at first he had held an acting contract and took no part in the early appointments. 'You begin with a shambles and it is hard to get back from it,' he said, in explanation of later problems. Doris, a loyal office assistant who respected Mr Wake, said that he considered himself fortunate to have got a headship, and a number of staff believed that he had worked well during the early days. Eleanor remembered that: '...he was very good when he was acting head when the school was first built, but when he got the permanency he seemed not to be'.

The school's organisation was unchanged during most of Mr Wake's time. According to the handbook the primary aim was to ensure 'that ours is a caring school.' Year heads and form tutors were responsible for mixed ability groups, while block timetabling 'allows for the adoption of setted groups, or smaller working groups within our support system, enabling the pupils to work at their best level in academic subjects' (Hillside Handbook). Stephen, a design technology teacher, was pleased that Mr Wake 'had a lot of time for the students, particularly ... lower achievers or students with social/ emotional problems ... he knew the children very well'. Eleanor confirms that 'he knew every kid's name ... in terms of being able to put his finger on a child.' Clive, the father of two children at the school who later became a governor and chair of the PAG, noticed that Mr Wake was prepared 'to accept disadvantaged students who were not wanted anywhere else'. Darren felt that Mr Wake was 'very reluctant to exclude pupils'.

Mr Wake emphasised his role in working with students. At the time of the inspection he taught for twelve contact periods and believed in delegating as much administration and management as he could. As he said: 'It seemed to me that the deputy who liked administration should do it.' When she became a deputy herself, Elaine saw the relationship rather differently:

> Mr Wake didn't run the school ... He had a very, very efficient and overworked and over-stressed deputy ... who did all the adminis-tration ... Mr Wake ... made final decisions if he felt like it.

Hillside's governors met infrequently and played no active role in the school. The head's report was tabled at termly meetings, rather than circulated in advance, and there were no standing orders to regulate the conduct of business, nor a committee structure. Clive later complained: 'The governors weren't even aware of being able to discuss school finances at any level. There was certainly no history of any direct involvement in the management of the school.'

Subject leaders were allowed the freedom to develop their depart-ments. Mr Wake believed that: 'You don't buy a dog and bark yourself'. Stephen found that while the head 'didn't interfere unless he was sort of disgruntled about something' there was never enough money for equipment and materials. Mr Wake warned his colleagues that 'you won't hear from me if it goes well; but I'll come down like a ton of bricks if you land me in it, make a mess.'

When long-serving members of staff recalled positive experiences, these had all been in the distant past. Stephen recalled that:

> We used to have things like school musicals and school plays and these ... I can't remember when these stopped, I suspect that might

have been when the union activity and the goodwill went out of the window ... I think things never really picked up from these and I think Mr Wake took it very personally ... if he could do it on his own, he would do it on his own.

Alan, a retired senior teacher, believed that Mr Wake's curmudgeonly outlook began with union action in the mid-1980s: 'He took everything personally, the industrial action he saw as against him.' Following a personal crisis, Mr Wake had 'lost his faith in human nature' and after that 'everything was too much trouble' and he would not allow 'things that would involve effort'.

When staff withdrew from dinner duties and extra-curricular activities as a result of the industrial action, Mr Wake assumed responsibility for lunchtime organisation and supervision. Eleanor remembered that 'there were strikes and nobody would do the dinner queues. He always did that.' Darren sensed that Mr Wake was 'battling against the staff' and that was why he retained personal control of lunch arrangements long after the industrial action was over:

> ...after ... the industrial action he took it upon himself to organise lunchtimes ... so he would stand at the front of the dinner queue getting all the kids through lunch ... if anything interrupted that or a child was late ... certainly the PE staff, we like to do practices at lunchtime ... he would go mad.

As a year head, Jean was disappointed when clubs, trips and visits were discouraged on the grounds that they disrupted the daily organisation, especially at lunchtime. Although students were locked out of the school, Stephen noticed that they 'still managed to find their way in through fire doors.' According to Jean there was 'raw antagonism between many but not all staff and pupils'.

Mr Wake's relationships with staff became increasingly negative. Stephen said that he became 'a bit of a dictator ... he described himself as a benevolent despot once' and reflected that if you 'put your hands up in the staff room who got on with him I don't think there would be many hands going up. He was quite a loner really and if you upset him he would come out with a few charged words.' Darren claimed that some people were afraid to speak at staff meetings:

> Mr Wake would speak for half an hour on a subject when holding staff meetings ... and he would just tell staff what we were doing ... you might say something and the reaction you would get from (him) would be quite negative.

There was a widespread belief that Mr Wake neglected his duties. Eleanor suspected that 'he didn't do half the paper work he should have done' and 'didn't go to any meetings that he should really to promote the name ... Its image was very poor – everybody thought it was a rough school.' Jean believed there 'was a lot of feeling that it didn't matter in years gone by what we did'.

Mr Wake was reluctant to conduct daily assembly. He sent off for inspection copies of almost every 'assembling' book that was published but commented: 'I didn't use them, mind, I did assemblies off the cuff, a bit of this and a bit of that, I told the vicar, I'm not qualified to lead prayer, didn't feel up to it.' According to Jean 'he always did the same assembly every year for Lent, inevitably the pupils' attention would wander'. Darren noticed that there were few assemblies and 'no assembly plan'.

Elaine was conscious that the year heads and subject teachers were frustrated by the head's sympathetic approach to disadvantaged and disruptive students:

> A lot of kids ceased to have any respect for him especially in disciplinary matters because they knew it would go nowhere ... as year heads we found the job extremely frustrating because we would come with what we thought were serious discipline problems and all he would do was bounce them back to us ... he couldn't be bothered.

Darren realised that 'Mr Wake would have parents of pupils in and say, look you are on your fifth last chance. Please buck your ideas up'. Consequently the heads of year lacked 'a higher referral. It was sort of take it to the headmaster and he would shelve it.'

As a parent herself, Anne was infuriated by the head's inconsistence:

> There have been other boys and girls that have been excluded for various reasons who were told they could not go on the end of term trip as part of their punishment. One boy came back after his

fixed-term exclusion and his parents came in to see the head to ask if the boy could go on the trip. The head said yes.

Hillside's social and cultural life seems not to have recovered from the impact of industrial action in the 1980s and many staff considered that Mr Wake did not communicate the school's values. Eleanor, later involved in the campaign to save the school from closure, reflected that in the past 'we were never in the paper for anything' while Stephen was unhappy because 'hardly anything got into the papers – he didn't want to know'. Clive thought that Mr Wake 'had limited vision' while staff and children interpreted bare walls and corridors as an absence of values. Jean agreed:

> The only thing you would see as you walked in – despite objections from the kids – was a stuffed animal in the display area, the emblem of the school.

According to Darren, who was keen to offer lunchtime activities:

> I think visitors saw very little going on at lunchtimes in terms of extra-curricular activities ...You would have seen some displays but [they were] very limited. You wouldn't have seen many staff around the school apart from duty teams ... the atmosphere was lukewarm.

Religious festivals like Diwali and Christmas were not celebrated. Elaine complained: 'We never had Christmas assemblies, Christmas didn't exist ... we have got Christmas celebrations planned this year – first time ever.' The reception area and office people were unwelcoming and Anne remembered 'complaints about their telephone manner and attitude to people'. Clive noticed 'a lack of care in the school about students' work – a lot of tatty wall displays including in one room that was often used for parents' evenings'.

Despite these concerns, most parents were happy. Elaine felt that as 'we were providing reasonable exam results ... overall parents thought that the school was doing OK by their kids'. Eleanor was aware that some parents were worried about the quality of teaching for the average and less academically able students. According to Anne, those from more socially advantaged, middle-class homes were perceived to be doing well at the school. In her opinion, the banded curriculum seemed to produce a 'big gap between the academic pupils and the SEN'. For many parents and teachers, Hillside seemed a definite success when compared with two neigh-bouring schools situated on large, deprived council estates. Governors, staff and a majority of the parents retained a positive view of the school, despite reservations about the head's personal style.

Clive recognised that 'teachers had a strong loyalty to the school. Perhaps a lump of this loyalty was that this was an easy place to work ... and incredibly overstaffed'. Many teachers were unaware of Hillside's inadequacies because in-service training and attendance at meetings at other schools were discouraged. Jean argues that the school was protected from reality by the head's determination to 'take no notice' of the outside world.

Shell shock night

A year before Hillside's Ofsted inspection, a county audit team con-ducted an evaluation of the school and submitted a critical report for the attention of the governing body. The audit found that 'the practice of locking some internal doors at lunchtime is an affront' and considered that 'reception and administrative staff are not effectively deployed to ensure good service'. According to the report, 'there was no evidence to suggest that a development planning cycle is in place' or that 'young people are encouraged to become involved in ... groups and activities'. Staff were found not to 'meet regularly with their managers to discuss their work or their pro-fessional development needs' and the audit team believed that 'fundamental changes in attitude and practice are needed' and that 'a similar process to that for a failing school be adopted' (Audit Report).

The report was not seen or considered by the governing body and the county team initiated no further action or enquiry. Mr Wake may have been encouraged by this experience to believe, as one teacher suggested, that he could 'treat the inspectors the way he treated us: waffle through'. As we have seen, the Ofsted inspection that November permitted few opportunities for 'waffle' (see Appen-dix, Table 1, p165). The inspectors found that 'the progress that significant numbers of pupils make is unsatisfactory ... Progress was judged to be unsatisfactory in almost 40 per cent of lessons at KS3 and KS4.' Attendance, at below 90 per cent, was reported to be unsatisfactory, while the 'quality of teaching varies widely across the school'. Mr Wake's personal responsibility was emphasised by the finding that: 'The leadership provided by the headteacher and governing body is ineffective as it does not promote high expectations or take a strategic view of the need to improve standards.' The report also pointed out that 'the workloads and responsibilities of the senior management team are distributed unevenly and some individuals carry an undue burden'. Hillside lacked 'effective strategic planning procedures' and employed an unsustainable number of teachers:

> A significant amount is now being spent on maintaining staffing levels. At the current rate of spending the school will exhaust its reserves within two years but there are no plans in place to review staffing.

Inspectors also rejected the 'widely held view that the standards of attainment of the intake are low and have fallen over the last few years. This view is not borne out by the evidence provided from the results of statutory assessment.'

According to the registered inspector, Mr Wake received the oral debrief without comment, apart from a grunt of dissent when the location of the science block was praised. During a subsequent interview he claimed that he knew the school would fail by the Tuesday evening of inspection week and believed that 'nothing we did after that would make a difference'. The inspection team was based on the county's advisory service and in his opinion included individuals who were collecting evidence to get rid of him. For many teachers, however, the inspection was a traumatic experience, followed by the blow of the school being placed in special measures.

Staff learned that the school had failed from the teacher representatives who attended the registered inspector's oral report to the board of governors, almost a week after the head had received the news. One of the teacher governors remembered that it had been 'shell shock night'. Jean suspected 'this was a shock to the staff because the academic work in the school was better than in other local schools'. Clive believed 'staff were demoralised because they thought the Ofsted report unfair'.

Almost at once Darren heard 'lots of rumours about how the inspection was geared towards trying to get rid of Mr Wake ... they already had an agenda to get rid of him'. A head of department claimed that the head's uncooperative attitude had caused the inspection team to arrive with a 'hidden agenda' which involved gathering evidence to discredit him and the school. Jean remarked that Mr Wake had been 'really very antagonistic to Ofsted' and that 'most of the inspectors in the team were from the LEA and they already knew the problems before the inspection'. She felt 'very wronged when the LEA inspection team put us in special measures. I felt we had been abandoned by our local authority.' Darren picked up resentment that Mr Wake had done so little to prepare them for inspection:

> He wasn't present in these sort of meetings so really ... we never saw our leader through the week ... he was out for much of the Ofsted week ... If he were truthful he would probably say that he didn't do enough to prepare us for inspection. During the Ofsted inspection things were very tense ... he was quite rude about the registered inspector ... sort of implying he didn't know what he was talking about. He said I'm not going to have people coming here telling me what to do.

In retrospect, Elaine felt they 'were playing a game completely blindfold. The only information we had was from members of staff who maybe had partners who had been through an inspection ... none of us knew what to expect.' Reactions to the inspection process were varied but Darren noticed that 'a lot of teachers were very tense and almost took things personally'. Eleanor reports that one of the special needs team was upset by an inspector who 'based all her judgement on withdrawal on about eight minutes observation ... and was very rude'. This teacher left Hillside within a few months. David, a geography teacher, was tearful when talking about the experience over a year later:

> I've not got over it, I'm sure they said positive things but she destroyed me, I've lost all my confidence, I doubt what I'm doing, I thought it was alright ... I've lost my way.

Mr Wake's reaction was that: 'I've always been able to walk away from it, I always said I'd stop when I stopped enjoying it.' But others realised that the school could not continue as it was. Darren noted: 'Mr Wake had no concrete structures to get us out ... He was saying that we should not have failed it anyway. But everybody else was saying ... what are you doing to solve these problems?' After an unsatisfactory meeting with him, staff forum wrote 'to express its great concern that there is a lack of commitment on the head's part to lead us successfully through any Special Measures, as proposed by Ofsted'. The letter was copied to the chair of governors. When Mr Wake met with the staff again a few days later Darren found that the mood was angry:

> People were saying ... 'we failed Ofsted. It's his fault' ... There was a motion of no confidence proposed ... and that this should be offered to the governors.

In the event the staff drafted a statement and voted with nine abstentions to send it to the governing body:

> Following the head's statement of intent in the last staff meeting we doubt his ability to change his present style of management to one which would be suited to carrying the school forward. The implementation of the proposed action plan would require effective and strong leadership. This, we feel, cannot be offered by the present principal.

The next day the chair of governors visited the school and met with Mr Wake and then with his deputy. He wrote to the county's personnel consultant:

> We should accept, with thanks for his past performance and dedication, the anticipated request from the deputy to take early retirement from Easter ... We should also accept Mr Wake's expected decision to take retirement from Easter, which I have requested he announces before the end of this term.

Mr Wake did not comply with this request to announce his resignation before Christmas. A county adviser was drafted in to assist the staff in preparing the required statutory action plan, while a personnel consultant continued to work with the chair of governors to secure the departure of the head, who had ceased to play an active role in the school. The Ofsted report was eventually published in January and Mr Wake's resignation followed shortly afterwards. The chair of governors persuaded him to 'accept absence with full pay and conditions' from the end of February, clearing the ground for the arrival of a temporary head drafted in from another school. As Darren remembered:

> Mr Wake walked into morning staff briefing in his confident manner and said at the end ... 'oh, by the way some of you will be very pleased to know that as of a month's time I am resigning'.

The decision by three other members of the senior management team to seek early retirement at the same time did not assist work on the action plan. The deputy was shattered by the outcome of the inspection. According to Anne 'the poor bloke was physically worn out by the time Ofsted had finished because everything was left to him.' The deputy interpreted the inspection outcome as a stain on his professional work and reported that it was over a year before he could sleep and concentrate normally again. The governors also agreed to release two senior teachers at the end of term, so that within four months of the inspection the school was left without experience or expertise in any aspect of senior management.

Task groups were established at the training day in January. One group aimed to develop and research a range of strategies for improving attendance and punctuality. A variety of objectives were listed, including 'to devise a systematic way of monitoring attendance and punctuality to include more pastoral meetings'. The recommendation was made that one person should be in overall charge of attendance. Another group was asked to review Hillside's management structure and it was proposed that 'patterns of management in other schools' should be looked at. The qualities of 'good management' were identified and included 'consultation, consideration, cooperation ... and consistency of approach' – all qualities Mr Wake was said to lack. As staff worked on the action plan they unconsciously succeeded in identifying many of the reasons why it was difficult for the school to move forward without new leadership.

Closure?

The action plan was completed and presented to the parents. Brian Goodlad, the acting head seconded from another school to replace Mr Wake for the summer term, said at the meeting he saw Hillside as 'a good school that could be an excellent school.' Meanwhile, the chair of governors wrote to the director of education for Easton, the newly created LEA that would take over responsibility for the school on April 1st, to request permission to advertise for a permanent head. The director's response was unexpected. He invited the chair of governors to an urgent meeting at which he announced the authority's intention to close Hillside. According to Clive, the LEA intended to close three local schools and open a new school on another site in order to take surplus places out of the system. Two years later an Ofsted inspection of the LEA summarised the position that faced the new local authority:

> There was a backdrop of falling rolls, with over 6,800 surplus places. The largest proportion of these surplus places (3,900) is in the secondary sector.

Elaine's theory was that the 'new authority felt that the focus was somewhat on them to do something about the problem ... The bright idea was that they would close all three, raise two phoenixes from the ashes on two sites.' Darren was impressed by the speed with which word of the threatened closure spread. All hell broke loose: 'the TV cameras were outside, radio, everybody wanted to be interviewed'. Eleanor later remembered a parents' meeting at the school in March:

> There were a lot of parents there and governors. At the end the deputy head asked any parents to stay behind who were interested because he announced that the threat of school closure was very unfair ... unjust but the fight against it was winnable.

The closure threat galvanised the community in support of the school, despite its recent Ofsted report. Jean observed that 'parental activism of whatever sort was started when the three school review was announced and a group of parents got together and decided that they weren't having that'. The level of commitment impressed Darren:

> As soon as the parents found out that this school would be possibly closed down they decided ... to get involved more in trying to save it. This school is probably one of the most popular in the area for the Asian families. They ... said that school is too good ... our kids are not that bad.

Parents at the meeting protested that Hillside was by far the most successful of the three nominated for closure. They were suspicious that the council had a hidden agenda to sell off the valuable Hillside site and to protect itself from the bad publicity it was about to receive for being the local authority with the greatest number of failing schools in the country. The PAG was founded on the spot. Led by Clive, who had previous experience of local campaigns, parents and a few teachers launched themselves into action. SEN teacher Eleanor was carried along by the general enthusiasm:

> We were all chucking money in buckets to raise finance ... we all ran round to get as many kids as possible to the education offices ... and Clive would tell us when the next council meeting was and how many people he wanted there ... or can we ring so many councillors?

Clive organised an intensive lobby, mobilising hundreds of parents, staff and students to appear at council meetings, write letters, make phone calls and besiege local politicians. In their newsletter they made their objective clear:

> All this is designed to achieve the simple objective of persuading the Council to rethink by making sure that they are in no doubt that Hillside has very strong support from its parents – and will not be easily closed down. Will we win? YES – we are determined that nothing will get in the way. We will not allow the Council to sacrifice a good school to solve problems which are none of our making.

Several sticks of gelignite
The LEA had asked Mr Goodlad to become acting head of a school in special measures during the summer term but the ink was no sooner dry on his contract than he discovered the director's plan was to close Hillside. Anne remembered:

> He agreed to take over a school in special measures, and had already accepted the post when the LEA earmarked the school for closure. This upset Mr Goodlad because he wanted to keep the school open. It led to conflict with the LEA.

Elaine later recalled: 'He got a phone call just before he was due to arrive at the school, saying 'actually it's not quite like that, we are going to close it' and his job was changed completely, from what I can make out.' Darren sensed that 'he had not applied for a school that was going to be closed down ... It just wasn't his brief at all. He had applied to try to get a school out of special measures and help create the development plan.' As PAG chair, Clive recognised the awkward position in which the new acting head found himself:

> Hillside was threatened with closure. It was not clear whether Mr Goodlad was appointed to achieve an orderly closure, but he thought he was appointed to turn the school around.

Clive felt that Mr Goodlad had been brought in as an expert by the LEA but then found himself caught up in the campaign to save the school. Clive was also deeply suspicious because the 'local council had already shown itself quite clearly to be unprincipled in terms of the way they were prepared to do things.' Elaine felt that the acting head 'never knew what game he was playing from one week to the next.'

When Mr Goodlad arrived at the beginning of March, Hillside's predicament was grim. The head and deputy had retired, together with two senior teachers who had been responsible for most of the administration. The school was in special measures and had been named for closure. The new LEA seemed an adversary rather than a source of support. Darren believed people were near despair because 'their jobs were on the line' but within a few days there was more bad news. Ofsted rejected the action plan prepared with the help of the county adviser, on the grounds that it paid too little attention to the key issues identified in the inspection report.

Clive was delighted with the new acting head, who came across as 'a very loveable man ... incredibly open, excitable, boyish, lots of humour, loads of energy and *joie de vivre*'. Anne thought he was 'an enthusiast who very quickly got to know what people could do'. Jean noticed that staff and students alike were swept along by his enthusiasm. Elaine thought he had 'a real common touch ... he can talk to anybody, he is quite happy to mutter on to anybody and the kids really like that about him, they could identify with him.' The caretaker said 'we were waiting for somebody like him really to take over which he did, encourage everybody because of his personality ... He's got the charm, you know.'

Darren thought 'he could have sold sand to the Arabs ... he oozed confidence ... He had the gift of convincing people to what he wanted ... so he had already come up with a solution but he was trying to make it out as if we staff were involved.' Clive realised that although he was mostly seen as 'a fantastic motivator' others 'had to be convinced ... that their efforts were going to be rewarded'. Elaine remarked that:

> ...not everybody took to him ... other people felt that he was a bit like several sticks of gelignite being set off at one time ... From years and years of nothing happening, you know, to Mr Goodlad with stuff going off all right, left and centre, and I don't think they found that easy to deal with.

Eleanor said that he had the gift of making people feel valued, which was especially important at a time when all the staff were aware of the threat to the school and their jobs. Passion and praise were prominent at morning briefing, and Anne soon noticed his use of the term 'brilliant' to describe almost any constructive effort. He was also prepared to 'push aside people who were not competent, like the bursar. He wanted quick results.' Stephen was concerned about the pace of change but he acknowledged that although Mr Goodlad had swept in and upset a lot of people, 'he did apologise before he upset anybody – a collective apology, you know, I am very sorry, I am going to upset a lot of you but I have got to do a lot of things fast.'

Clive thought the acting head 'was a bull in a china shop ... I think he was working at the intuitive level ... there was no time for calm reflection'. But Mr Goodlad believed he was clear and consistent in the pursuit of his stated objective:

> I aimed to challenge the staff through the students, they were at the centre of everything. I got them together in the hall and asked them what was wrong with the place. I wanted to use them to generate a buzz. Their energy would save the school.

Opening moves

Mr Goodlad told Elaine that 'if we were going down then we were going down fighting'. He worked with the staff and the PAG to bring about 'amazing changes' in the shortest possible time. Jean recalls that within days of his arrival at Hillside, he had introduced a daily staff briefing to get 'people involved for the first time.' For students, too, there were now daily assemblies and a student council was set up to work on a new behaviour code for the school. Jean saw that 'students responded well to his dynamism and to his assemblies. Suddenly they were being asked questions and they were being asked what they wanted.' Anne noticed that Mr Goodlad stressed the importance of students in the school and treated them 'as equals: pleasant and polite to them, and formed a student council'. Darren remembers that the new head also 'promised each child ... would get a locker, and vending machines ... drinks machines, chocolate machines'. The chains that had secured the main entrance at lunchtime were symbolically cut and students were allowed to remain indoors if they chose. As a result, clubs and societies began to come back.

Mr Goodlad also spent the £100,000 surplus that had built up in the school budget, appointing a number of teachers to temporary middle level management posts to help improve the quality of learning and teaching. Five internal candidates, three of them heads of year in receipt of two point allowances, were interviewed for two temporary deputy headships. One deputy was to be responsible for the 'quality and consistency of teaching', while the other would lead the 'monitoring and evaluation of pupil progress'. Elaine and Peter were the successful candidates and they joked that their leap from head of year to deputy head had led to a degree of 'altitude sickness'.

Some teachers were embittered when they missed out on the cascade of temporary points. A science teacher said later: 'Do you know I'm the only member of this staff who hasn't been promoted?' Stephen thought that Mr Goodlad 'was in too much of a rush' with his staff changes:

> He decided that various people were doing different jobs and instead of discussing them with the people who were actually doing it at the moment, they would arrive at the door and find that 'you are not doing that job any more'.

Within weeks, work started on a new reception area. Although critical of the expense and haste, Stephen also appreciated the symbolism of building a smart, modern extension:

> Mr Goodlad came in to try and convince everybody that this place isn't closing and also I think it was a big morale-boosting job for the staff as well. Who in their right minds would spend whatever thousand pounds that cost on a school that was going to close?

A major upheaval in the offices followed. Stephen, who was also head of careers, protested that he was

> ...kicked out with nowhere to go ... Then I was given a classroom and now I am actually in the laundry room, which is horrendous. So I have got a careers office, trying to interview students, and there is a washing machine clattering away in the background.

Clive welcomed this burst of activity that immeasurably strengthened the campaign. He acknowledged that 'there was no way that I could be out there defending the school on moral and political grounds alone'. Elaine saw that although the PAG was 'self-started by the parents ... with Mr Goodlad's support and help a lot of parents came on board from a whole different range of backgrounds'. Darren watched the campaign grow. Assemblies were used to encourage students 'to write to the local authorities to lobby and make petitions ... to the right people ... Quite a hefty proportion of our students took up the fight with a lot of the parents.' The PAG also helped to raise morale in the school. The emergence of powerful parental support made the teachers really want to work hard to keep the place open.

One hundred parents lobbied councillors at the LEA Education Committee meeting on April 7. A proposal to stage a three-school review, instead of closing them without further consultation, was referred to the full council meeting on April 24. When the full council met to consider the plan,

> Nearly three hundred parents, teachers and children met outside the town hall to demonstrate support for the school. A 700-name petition, prepared by pupils, was presented to the chair of Education ... who ... refused to say whether the Director had stated that he intended to recommend closure of Hillside before announcing his review. (PAG Bulletin)

The campaign to save the school moved into a new phase when the pressure failed to shift enough votes. It was vital to persuade the council that common justice required that all Easton secondary schools be reviewed, not just the three that happened to be in special measures. As PAG chair, Clive secured the support of the local MP, while Mr Goodlad was determined to make the school look good and invited the press to a series of public events.

In June, Hillside staged an open day that featured the MP, guided tours of the school, demonstrations of the newly installed computer suite, exhibitions of students' work, sports, activities, sideshows and refreshments. Jean was pleased with the result:

> When the parents decided that an open day would be a good thing, suddenly wall displays began to go up all over the place. It was very successful with the people from the local community and helped to raise the school's profile.

A fortnight later, Clive wrote to Stephen Byers, Minister of State for Education, arguing the school's case for survival and emphasised 'the very real parental and community support for Hillside':

> The result of the Ofsted inspection, and the council's reaction, has been rather like letting the cork out of the bottle: parents have now found a voice and have made that voice heard very loudly indeed.

Shortly afterwards, the council dropped the decision to close the three schools. Members voted instead for a two-year long review of all Easton secondary schools. Mr Goodlad wrote to Hillside parents with the good news that a breathing space had been won:

> The threat of imminent closure is now over ... the authority wide review will take at least two years to fulfil. We intend to take full advantage of this situation to put our Action Plan into operation and prove that Hillside is a highly successful and thriving school. Already we have reached targets that we had set for next year ... our ... results are all in line with, or above national expectations and we await the GCSE results in August with confidence.

Although Mr Goodlad seemed to work intuitively and in Elaine's opinion could explode in all directions at once 'like several sticks of gelignite being set off at one time', his approach to drafting a new action plan to replace the original one that Ofsted rejected was formal and systematic. Anne typed the plan as he paced up and down his office dictating. Elaine noted that the document 'was taking quite a lot of his time.' Clive recognised Mr Goodlad's dilemma:

The school had to create a new action plan very quickly and Mr Goodlad did it mainly himself, because of the low chances of getting staff to agree to work on it again after the failure of their first effort.

Mr Goodlad organised the action plan so that the four key target areas for action exactly matched the key issues identified by Ofsted inspectors. He set out in a matrix the planned steps towards improved management, higher expectations, better teaching, raised standards and the more efficient use of resources. The main actions were:

- a new, permanent head as well as the two deputies to be appointed

- a new management structure to be established

- pupil progress and curriculum teams to be created

- regular meetings to be established

- homework, attendance, punctuality, attitudes, behaviour and personal development to be monitored and improved

- lesson observation, appraisal, consultancy and training to be used to eliminate inconsistencies in teaching

- the student council, computers, lockers and cultural celebrations would be introduced to improve the school's ethos

- the pupil teacher ratio to be increased from 1:14 to 1:18

- all spending decisions to be analysed

- the use of support staff to be reviewed.

Mr Goodlad convened a staff weekend conference at a local hotel before he finalised and submitted the action plan he had prepared. Determined to return to his own school at the end of term, Mr Goodlad also drafted an Action Plan Timetable as a checklist for his successor and the senior managers who would be responsible for achieving the targets he had set. The timetable showed what had to be done by whom and set deadlines for each action. Middle management job descriptions were to be revised in April, for example, while office arrangements were to be reviewed by the end of May and a scheme for reporting to parents on pupil progress was to be in place by June.

Mr Goodlad resisted pressure to stay at Hillside and implement his plan. He wished to return to his old place, where he said his heart lay. The governors had no alternative but to commission their personnel consultant to search for another temporary head, because the LEA would not allow any headship appointments during the two-year review period. Hillside and other schools might still be closed. Names were canvassed, phone calls were made and interested parties came to visit. By the day in June set aside for interviews, only two candidates remained. One would have to be seconded from another school; the other was a recently retired head from a neighbouring authority. The governors opted for Chris Moore, an experienced headteacher who had contacted the LEA after seeing the vacancy advertised in the *Times Educational Supplement*. Mr Moore accepted a two-year contract, to commence at the start of the autumn term.

In his diary, Mr Moore recorded everyone's joy when the examination results came out that summer:

> Great excitement because the results have improved from 27 per cent 5+ A*-Cs to 40 per cent, placing Hillside near the head of the local averages and perhaps high in the list of 'most improved' schools nationally. Terrific public relations material and a boost for staff and students. There was a lovely atmosphere in the foyer with excited and surprised young people and some of their parents. As Brian Goodlad didn't arrive almost until the students were on study leave it is hard to see how the action plan has contributed; but what has? Demoralisation and fear seem to have done the trick? Or a lucky twist of fate with a known 'good' year group? But Brian has the credit and deservedly so, because he has injected confidence, optimism and hope, although moving so fast I suspect there will be a lot of details for dogged me to pick up, not least the lunch supervision arrangements and the office imbroglio.

In retrospect, Elaine tried to assess Mr Goodlad's contribution:

> If you look at it in terms of trying to personify the school as some kind of being – Brian Goodlad described it as a 'sleeping giant' – well, it was a very quietly sleeping giant and it was a very quietly

sleeping disgruntled giant in that it really didn't care ... whereas this wasn't a sleeping giant that it was up and awake and moving about and doing good things. It was lively and there was evidence that the kids wanted to be involved ... staff were being encouraged to follow their own 'yellow brick roads'.

Brian Goodlad could not forget that after the LEA had placed him in the school, he had been abandoned. The promised extra support had never materialised and he had been caught up in an impossible turmoil. In a letter to the LEA, Clive protested that: '...no support was made available during the critical period of Mr Goodlad's leadership'. The LEA denied the charge but could identify no help beyond that available to all its schools.

4

Fireworks

New head

Chris Moore's arrival at Hillside was reported in the *Easton Morning Post* under the headline 'New head vows to help rescue school'. It quoted his promise 'to continue an improvement in exam results to prevent the school being closed.' The school had been:

> ...threatened with closure after a poor Ofsted report last year. But an action plan, put into place by the former head, Mr Brian Goodlad, has seen a turn-around at the school with the proportion of pupils gaining five or more C-grade GCSE passes rising from 27 per cent last year to 40 per cent this summer.

Mr Moore did not discourage this interpretation of the examination results and asserted that: 'It's difficult to close a school where standards are improving.' Although Hillside would be part of a general reorganisation within a year, he did not believe the school would close.

Both Brian Goodlad and Chris Moore projected self-confidence to the public and courted the local media. Although they earned the respect of colleagues – who noticed the school had been in the press more times in the last twelve months than in the last ten years – both were well aware of the school's vulnerability. Over twenty per cent of the student roll was lost in the five months between April and September. Clive said that most of those who left were the 'children whose parents were most concerned about their education' and Jean agreed that it was mainly the most able academic students who were taken away. The transfer from primary partner schools was down by a third, reflecting fears that if Hillside closed, the children would have to go to other local schools that were also in special measures. Not one student transferred from the school's largest designated primary partner that September. The financial implications of such a catastrophic mid-year loss of numbers were equally serious, particularly as Gerald, the bursar, had stopped working during the summer.

Mr Moore calculated that the staff had to be won over before there was a chance of sustained recovery and planned to build confidence through a speedily established new discipline system. As an experienced head, he knew the importance of being seen to support teachers and decided, in advance, to search for three or four permanent exclusions to back staff and send the message that poor behaviour would not be tolerated. In his diary he concluded that a 'high energy, high profile, high impact strategy should work'. He planned an open forum at least once a week where all information and developments could be shared and the school's problems could be brainstormed. It was to be 'as unlike traditional staff meetings as possible'. A retired deputy from another school was commissioned to audit the school's finances and stabilise the current budget.

Mr Moore spent his first morning at Hillside on the telephone, speaking with various companies that were pursuing the school for unpaid bills:

> Gerald has made a point by not turning up in the holiday and no one else has the computer codes or knows how to work the system, especially in this case as some building tax or other applies.

After further enquiries he concluded: 'Gerald is disempowered and can't do the job; others don't know how to do it.' The bursar then had several periods of absence during the autumn before long term sickness overcame him. When he was at work, he complained bitterly about Mr Goodlad's 'unnecessary' changes. Mr Moore realised that the support staff were 'unhappy and resentful' because of that summer's hurried reorganisation. Mr Goodlad had embarked on a massive programme of change but had neglected important details in favour of big gestures.

Mr Goodlad set out to isolate both Gerald, whom he thought incompetent, and Sidney, a long-serving senior teacher he believed to be untrustworthy and uncooperative. He had moved the senior teacher to a small office at the end of a corridor, and disconnected his telephone and computer. During the holiday, Sidney returned all the furniture and equipment to his old office and stirred discontent amongst the secretarial staff. Mr Goodlad's management restructuring had brought new people into administrative positions and swept aside remnants of the old order like Sidney, whose post as Head of Lower School simply disappeared. And at the last moment, the LEA refused to fund his redundancy.

Mr Moore was invited to attend the PAG celebration buffet and met with parents and staff who were still excited by their success in winning a stay of execution. He found them friendly and keen to improve the school. Elaine, now newly appointed curriculum deputy, believed that the PAG had won the battle over closure and was now developing a new role, monitoring the local authority review of secondary education.

Immediate problems with budgets and telephones did not deflect Mr Moore from his determination to consolidate Mr Goodlad's changes and 'to make sure what is agreed happens.' He recognised the statutory status of the action plan approved by Ofsted just before his arrival and understood that it would be impossible to change any substantive objective:

> I've gutted the action plan now and feel more or less in command of it and able to anchor my own thoughts in it and my own early priorities are equally clear – support staff, lunch supervision, awkward senior teacher, revised time structure, staff training for the classroom.

Mr Moore used the two training days at the beginning of his first term to establish an agreed framework for developing, monitoring and evaluating lessons. A set of lesson guidelines and three lesson transcripts were distributed and teachers were asked to use their experience and the guidelines to consider whether the selected lesson matched their expectations of good practice. The aim of the workshop was to develop a common approach to lesson planning, preparation and classroom teaching so that 'we impress inspectors and other visitors with our shared strategy' and 'match Ofsted criteria and expectations'.

A lesson plan strategy was agreed, whereby everyone would prepare their lessons to emphasise learning objectives and the new, common approach. Jean commented:

> Mr Moore made it very clear what was expected of us ... he set lesson plans where we had to identify our learning objectives ...We were taught to teach in a certain style ... and we would all start the lesson in the same way.

Mr Moore explained that his approach was to explain what changes were needed, rather than demand unthinking obedience. On the whole, teachers welcomed this method. Darren explained the startling contrast between the heads:

> ...we had been taught the command style of teaching by Mr Wake but Mr Moore is about 'get a partner, discuss, talk about, see what things you can come up with' ... he is very up to date on things that are going on.

At his first assembly with the students the following morning, Mr Moore chose to announce his decision not to go ahead and install the vending machines that had been ordered. He was responding to the concerns of the catering staff, who were worried about their jobs, and he also wanted to please the teachers who were worried about supervising unruly queues. Stephen was reassured:

> I think the children thought he was the best thing since sliced bread because suddenly lockers appeared ... the drinks machine was on offer, which I thought was a foolish thing – but he disappeared before that came along and Mr Moore decided it wasn't a good idea, which I was relieved at.

Mr Moore cancelled the installation of drinks and chocolate machines, mainly because the canteen boss, Pam, was unhappy, but also because he wanted to signal a changed approach:

> I announced the drinks stoppage in assembly which prompted a response only from the older pupils. I also challenged their lack of uniform.

Teachers welcomed the new head's firmness with the students. Darren noted that: 'Mr Moore came in and said he didn't want the vending machines and so he was instantly unpopular.' Mr Moore reflected on the difference between Mr Goodlad's stance and his own: 'He is very student centred, uses them to challenge the staff; I'm more of a cautious politician, handling the staff like an electorate.'

When dealing with the first few students referred to him because of their repeatedly violent misbehaviour, Mr Moore rigorously applied the behaviour code that had been developed during the summer term. Elaine believed such clarity was important:

> We have a code of conduct that we keep referring to, that they had a hand in dealing with and putting together. They know that there is a discipline procedural referral system and they know where referrals will go and how they will be dealt with ... they see a clear line of command.

Jean noticed the impact on the students:

> ...on the whole I think student behaviour has improved. People are dealt with more efficiently than they were and more fairly. It is the same rule for all, rather than one rule for one and one rule for another as it was under the old regime.

Clive thought there were fewer children out of class because 'they've tightened up on procedures ... A lot of them used to go to the sick room with a headache.'

Although Mr Moore could be ruthless in eliminating longstanding, unresolved cases, he was fully aware of the competing priorities involved in dealing with troublesome students:

> Mrs Smith knows Jade needs help; tells me that Jade used to attack other children out of the blue even when very young ... I suggest that permanent exclusion might provoke a sufficient crisis to get her special education ... But the risk of readmitting her and allowing her to carry on stirring trouble and punching those concerned? Jade's eyes roll; she has an angry core and it could be very dangerous in time ... But why has this not been referred ... before? ...Our provision for children with acute problems is awful and we leave headteachers to agonise over whether or not to sacrifice individuals for the good of the whole ... I don't think Jade can stay.

> She is beyond what teachers can do for her already. She doesn't want to be in school; learning is the last thing on her mind.

Jade was excluded, despite Mr Moore's reservations, and the staff welcomed her swift departure and the exclusion of several other seriously disruptive students who had not been dealt with during the summer turbulence. He was anxious to create a climate where learning is possible and wanted teachers to 'feel that I am backing them in their relations with the children'. Jean said the year heads in particular appreciated the arrival of a head who took an active role in student discipline:

> I think that the children are aware of the structures. They are aware that there is a line and that they can be suspended ... and that could lead to permanent exclusion.

Darren saw the change in simple terms:

> When Mr Moore came in he identified a few troublemakers and got rid of a few and sent the message out that 'we are not standing for this.' Mr Moore came in and made an immediate impact.

Roles and responsibilities

The two temporary deputy heads appointed by Mr Goodlad were at the centre of Mr Moore's plan to establish roles and responsibilities for everyone. The departure of the long-standing permanent deputy the previous spring meant that no one was now looking after basic routines. Elaine, who was responsible for the curriculum and Peter, who was in charge of pupil progress, had set to work to establish effective systems, although gaps remained, as Mr Moore noted in his diary:

> As positive comments flow I'm beginning to realise how much the deputies have achieved. They've been inventing and introducing systems for five months and I have to admire Mr Goodlad's vision in appointing them.

Mr Moore agreed to meet with them every morning at 8.00 am to plan and monitor progress and led after-school training to help them learn the techniques of budget and curriculum analysis. Elaine recalled:

...we have been in on everything and he has involved us in every-thing and he has actually asked our opinion and consulted us on things which has felt nice because it seems like he respects us as individuals.

The deputies were eager to learn and impressed Mr Moore with their professional commitment. He soon saw that Elaine and Peter inspired an 'extraordinary degree of staff confidence and trust' and acknowledged the importance of their role:

...having really credible people inside the school doesn't half build up the confidence of the rest ... they have done a wonderful job in carrying the staff through what's been an absolutely diabolical ex-perience.

He decided to make their posts permanent so they would be able to help others cope with the rough ride ahead without 'their own posi-tion being vulnerable' and to ensure a bridge between himself and the staff. According to Elaine:

Mr Moore decided that he wanted some stabilising influences so he effectively made Peter and myself permanent – he wanted two permanent deputies.

The three were soon working closely together, taking decisions, pre-paring initiatives and providing mutual support. Mr Moore con-sidered 'the quality of leadership of the two deputies and the level of trust they have from the other staff is ... the core of the school's development' and delegated major responsibility to them. Anne noticed that Mr Moore worked closely with Elaine and Peter:

I think he feels that the more decisions that can be made jointly the better. It takes the work off him. For example, one of the deputies is in charge of the curriculum and goes to governors' committees.

After personal discussions with members of Mr Goodlad's tem-porary senior management team, Mr Moore drafted a scheme that placed each deputy or senior teacher in charge of a governor com-mittee, a staff working group and a key issue in the Ofsted action plan. The retired deputy head brought in by Mr Moore to sort out the budget imbroglio was offered a temporary part-time contract to lead on finance and manage improvements to the site and build-ings. Objectives and outcomes were prescribed and tabulated.

Elaine, the curriculum deputy was responsible for example for drafting a school calendar for the year and for leading a working group to review the curriculum. Her task was to increase the pupil-teacher ratio and broaden the curriculum. Her targets were specified in the action plan. Peter, who was in effect the pastoral deputy, was responsible for the heads of year and for ensuring that the new behaviour code was properly established. In addition to the pupil progress targets specified in the action plan, including those for homework and attendance, Peter was required to devise a tutorial programme for almost immediate implementation and to set up a lunch supervision scheme which had not been completed over the summer as it should have been.

Graham, a temporary senior teacher, was made responsible for training, daily cover and the spiritual, moral, social and cultural dimension that had been criticised in the Ofsted inspection report. Graham led a working group and organised a series of public events, from daily assembly to multicultural festivals. Staff appreciated Graham's ability to delegate effectively and to ensure that tasks are moved forward and completed. A new teacher said: 'He's been fantastic for me as an NQT, he sent me maps, helped with my CV.' Donna, another temporary senior teacher, was put in charge of press, publications and presentation. Although Graham and Donna worked tirelessly, they were also responsible for substantial departmental and pastoral responsibilities, and this compromised their ability to operate as full members of the senior team.

The Head's Report to Governors detailed the progress of the four working parties led by senior management:

> The Communication Group has ... produced a ... Guide for Parents, an advertising supplement for the *Easton Herald* ... and ... displays throughout the school ... I have visited seven schools to meet with the heads and staff and have returned to most for an extended discussion with year five and year six students. Lack of communication ... has reduced our share of catchment area children.

> The Tutoring and Mentoring Group's ... task is to improve ... systems for monitoring and assisting student progress. They are designing a Record of Achievement as a focus for a number of developments, including the introduction of individual interviews

for all students, at which work is reviewed and targets for the future set. Performance information (e.g. GCSE results; SAT, CAT and reading test scores) is to be entered in a database so we can analyse our effectiveness in teaching and learning.

The Ethos group is concerned with celebration and aims to establish a revised assembly programme based on themes, a strong cultural dimension within the curriculum and a variety of events, including a Diwali evening on October 24, Christmas and other social functions. They want the texture of school life to be rich and rewarding so that everyone enjoys working at Hillside and feels valued. The most important of these planned events is the first ever Certificate Evening, to be attended by the Mayor and Brian Goodlad, who will present awards.

In order to implement the action plan promise, the Curriculum Group must increase the pupil-teacher ratio from 1:15 to 1:18, and teachers' contact time with pupils from 75 per cent to 80 per cent. In view of the serious loss of pupils since the budget was constructed in April this may be insufficient.

These new staff working groups joined with parents who had campaigned to save the school to stage numerous activities. When Mr Moore was told that: 'We never celebrate anything at Hillside', he decided to create a social calendar with a strong emphasis on doing things together and involving students. Led by Graham and the 'Ethos' group, teachers and parents launched themselves into a flurry of events. Elaine remarked on:

> ...all these clubs and activities that are going on at lunch times – the place is buzzing. There is stuff going on after school as well. People have been coming out of the woodwork with – can we run this activity, can I run a trip, can we go here? Can we do that?

Darren commented:

> There has been an awful lot of work on parents' evenings, presenting the school in a very positive way to parents ... slowly we are receiving a trickle of children from other schools.

According to Darren, there was a 'history club, a homework club, a chess club, a computer club, a design club and arts', and other teachers remarked on the new emphasis on the display of students' work. Jenny, the new head of humanities, who arrived at the same time as Mr Moore, commented: 'The kids love to see these displays ... I always put everybody's work up.' Stephen was pleased to see students 'who have said 'don't touch that, I've done that, don't you spoil that' ... which is quite nice to see happen'. People remembered the Diwali evening as the highlight of the term. Darren was encouraged to see so many events:

> We had a Diwali celebration that was open to parents, children ... it was a case of 'join us at our house to celebrate something we have in common' ... it was really successful ... next week there is to be some sort of Christmas extravaganza where they will put on a bit of a show in the evening for parents and pupils.

The caretaker helped arrange the hall for Diwali and was excited by the atmosphere that had been created:

> We had fireworks and everybody enjoyed themselves – we had lots of food – Indian food, you know, because we've got quite a lot of Indian children, you know, and it's nice to make them feel part of the community, you know.

Elaine was impressed with the skills that were revealed:

> We had no idea that they could do it and there were a lot of Asian girls who did Asian dancing and we have got an Asian science teacher so she trained the girls up and taught them how to do that ... they did sketches and poems.

Mr Moore regarded Hillside's dysfunctional office as an equally important priority and agreed with Elaine that: 'Until the administration is sound, nothing else will work'. He interviewed all the members of the support staff and identified concerns about the efficiency of almost every aspect of the school's administration. There was only one assistant to cope with all the business of the general office; no technical support was provided for the administrative and curriculum ICT networks; no learning support assistants were employed; and the old line management structure had broken down. There was no obvious rationale for grades, hours of employment or the allocation of responsibility.

Mr Moore's report on the review contained detailed proposals to solve these difficulties. He recommended replacing the old bursar with a new business manager; advised extending the role of head's secretary into that of a personal assistant, responsible for providing professional support to all members of the senior management team and redefined office roles and responsibilities. Additional posts were created to cover the gaps that had been identified, while all the administrative and support staff were assimilated to a common pay spine, with scales adjusted to the degree of responsibility held.

The governors approved the proposals in early October and the head proceeded to implement them at once, through a mixture of consultation, negotiation and advertisement. Gerald eventually and reluctantly accepted the redundancy that had been engineered for him and departed at Christmas, while everyone else slotted into the posts that had been created, accepting the detailed job descriptions prepared as part of the review.

As the governors had been criticised as 'ineffective' in the Ofsted inspection report, Mr Moore was not surprised when the clerk to the governors, a retired LEA official, informed him that there were 'no committees, no calendar, no procedures, no terms of reference' and that 'exclusion systems are non-existent'. He set to work with the chair of governors to produce a governance package that would ensure 'effective accountability through the governing body'. Each governor was attached to a year group and was expected to monitor progress in academic attainment; homework; attendance; punctuality; attitudes; behaviour; and personal development, gathering information by observing students and talking with tutors. Standing orders were established for meetings of the full governing body, while terms of reference were drafted for each of the five committees that would monitor the implementation of the action plan. Members of the senior management team were expected to support the chairs of the committees in managing their business effectively.

As he worked on these systems and structures, Mr Moore reflected that:

> When a headteacher doesn't communicate or bring people together, no one else can and fragmentation is the result. I think that's what's happened here. Already I'm pulling in the boundaries and making contacts with all the people who can help us; pulling the staff together to look for solutions.

Shell shocked

While interviewing the office staff, Mr Moore discovered that Sidney had been 'agitating' about the changes that were being made. He asked the senior teacher to explain his 'continuous stirring of negativity':

> He admitted to subversion of Mr Goodlad, he takes responsibility for nothing, blames the school or me for the absence of whatever and encourages an atmosphere of complaint and dissatisfaction.

Mr Moore administered an immediate oral warning, issued a revised job description and hired a consultant to assist Sidney with his new, strictly limited duties. A few weeks later Anne told Mr Moore that Sidney was encouraging the receptionist to leave the telephone unanswered. After another unproductive interview, the head issued a memorandum of meeting, and warned him that further misconduct would lead to formal disciplinary action. Sidney became ill and did not return to the school. A year later, his application for ill-health retirement was successful.

As the head began to implement his new structures, with their inevitable personnel implications, he found the LEA less than helpful. Hillside was at odds with the new director as a result of the events of the summer and according to Mr Moore the secondary review had added:

> ...a level of destabilisation to the relationships between the LEA and schools, within the schools and between the schools, so it's sort of implosion of boundary management, watching all the head-teachers at work, it's a nightmare. They're all trying to avoid something nasty happening to them.

Mr Moore was frustrated when:

> You ring the head of personnel, she's away for a couple of weeks but will get back to you – a month later she gets back to you to tell you, you want someone else, then that somebody tells you, you didn't want that in the first place.

The LEA was reluctant to fund Gerald's redundancy package and warned against taking action on Sidney's disruptive behaviour. Mr Moore felt that important lines of communication had ceased to work, and noted in his diary that: 'I don't feel I've got a working relationship with anybody, really. They don't talk to you, they don't communicate with you.'

As Hillside's internal systems and processes began to improve, the school's demand for advice and services seems to have increased beyond the LEA's ability to respond. Mr Moore wrote to the LEA director:

> We become increasingly dependent on the council to bring staffing and budgetary issues to a conclusion. Unless there is effective exit support, we are unable to remove unsatisfactory staff.

Two months later, having finally agreed to fund Gerald's departure, the LEA wrote to inform him that it had miscalculated his retirement package and demanded money back. No progress had been made in resolving the employment position of several teachers who had agreed to leave. When the LEA was inspected two years later, the official report confirmed that 'communication on specific issues relating to a school is poor' and noted that support for governing bodies was unsatisfactory. The LEA was urged to 'improve the effectiveness of its personnel services'.

Once his new schemes were written, Mr Moore embarked on individual development interviews with every member of staff. Elaine reported her perception of these exchanges:

> He has had a half hour/three quarters of an hour chat with everybody to build up a profile of each one of them so that they have had opportunities to talk to him one to one. I think they were quite blown away by him when they first met him, because he is quite impressive and I can remember the first time I met him, it was like being hit by a heavy blunt instrument. He has tried to be honest and straightforward.

Mr Moore's plan to improve the quality of teaching involved:

> Training in monitoring and evaluation to establish/agree a model lesson for Hillside; Consultancies with me on personal development; the message that I'll train them like hell to get through Ofsted hoops and that those who don't need training can help others who do.

His interviews with staff members did not entirely clarify how far stress and breakdown could be attributed to individual or school factors. He noted that '66 per cent of the teachers were found to be satisfactory, there are some outstanding teachers' and sympathised with the

> ...excellent people who never deserved to be caught up in the fiasco of a failing school ... who think they've failed in some way; who've been humiliated in public for their leader's faults ... they give themselves absolutely and unreservedly to the school.

But he also identified a group of teachers who had been recruited during the final phase of Hillside's decline, when the school had become unpopular with parents and was known locally to be an unwise career move:

> We have at least eight teachers whose careers have been seriously broken by redundancy, periods of unemployment, re-deployment or unintended absence from the job market.

After he had seen everyone, he reflected that 'there's a shortage of yuppies, nobody's ever gone anywhere for a very long time, people have forgotten what an interview is'.

His overall impression was that:

> People seem so defeated, so lacking in power that 'politics' is not really the word. They're not inert, they're very much together, but when I asked the consultative group about micro politics they immediately said: 'Smokers and non-smokers.'

During the personal interviews, Mr Moore heard stories that he struggled to interpret. William, for example, was an RE teacher, Mr Wake's last appointment:

> He describes his career in teaching – age 40 and he has been made redundant, reorganised and otherwise unfortunate over and over again, even beginning his career with three or four maternity leaves where the mother returned against expectations. Now his car has gone and he needs a loan and he's wondering whether his temporary post will last and is too old for a head of department and too junior for a deputy. He is an honest man and knows he's good at GCSE results and that's about it. He teaches in this open double bay with Richard and they listen to one another, video and lecture, day in, day out. My sense is that he's a worthwhile human being who has been horribly treated, just like almost everyone at Hillside.

A few were visibly distressed:

> ...one or two were in tears remembering the Ofsted experience.
> They're just gutted by it to the point of whatever nervous state they
> were in before Ofsted, it was much worse after.

Financial crisis

As the personal development interviews progressed, the head received a detailed report on the school's finances from the retired deputy head who had been brought in to investigate after Gerald's breakdown:

> The numbers have dropped by 20 per cent since the last budget
> was made. As a result, we're nearly £165,000 down. We could need
> to lose up to fourteen teachers.

Mr Moore decided to tell the staff, even though they would find the prospect of fourteen redundancies devastating, on the grounds that the news would leak out anyway. The strategic issue, however, was whether or not to tell the LEA. Should Hillside

> ...keep it to ourselves and perform heroic surgery in private in the
> hope of surviving and building up numbers slowly in future years;
> or talk it through with the LEA, providing perfect ammunition for
> closure? The figures prove what they want; not viable, too expen-
> sive, no children.

There was so much suspicion and mistrust between the school and the LEA that Chris Moore doubted whether there was sufficient common ground for a satisfactory solution. After a successful, well-attended open evening with greatly improved displays of students' work, he met with Clive, the PAG chair, to agree strategy. He then prepared a paper, entitled: 'Case Study: How to Destroy a School', that blamed the local authority for the budget crisis:

> As a direct result of the LEA's actions, Hillside has suffered a catas-
> trophic loss of pupils which has induced a serious financial crisis.
> No discussions have taken place as to how this may be resolved.

A week later Clive and the head decided the financial problem was unlikely to prove fatal. The action plan reductions might solve it, although there was no predicting the impact of the LEA reorganisation due the following year. They agreed to invite the LEA director to visit the school and to use the 'How to Destroy a School' paper as the focus for discussion and as 'possible blackmail' if the local authority refused to help.

Attending Staff Forum, a group that had aired complaints and grievances under Mr Wake and Mr Goodlad, made Mr Moore irritable, mainly because they 'raised lots of detailed complaints about things that don't work'. Later he reflected:

> I dislike the procedure they've lumbered themselves with ... they're genuine in working for the good of the school and not at all antagonistic or difficult. But I didn't try too hard to reassure ... I want them to think a bit about what staff forum is for and how it should relate to me.

He preferred the Consultative Group that he had established himself. It included union representatives, teacher governors and the chair of Staff Forum. Consultative Group members all held temporary promotion points and had been active in the campaign to save the school. He explained the school's dilemma and promised that when the teaching structure was revised and reduced in the spring, no process for filling posts or identifying redundancies would be adopted without their agreement. He knew this was 'a rash promise, but I'm determined to manage the internal reorganisation and restructuring so that there is the least possible damage'.

Chris Moore used the daily staff briefing, Staff Forum, the Consultative Group and senior management meetings to explain the circumstances of each major decision or development (e.g. budget reductions, curriculum changes, staff structure, secondary review, HMI monitoring) so that his colleagues had time to assimilate and understand what was happening. He believed that keeping staff 'on board and keeping them happy was a very, very important objective'.

All these groups agreed to what Mr Moore described as a re-launch after half-term. The working day would be adjusted so that there was time for tutorial work, using a set of materials to be provided by Graham. An assembly scheme would be introduced so that a variety of moral and spiritual themes could be included, while in future all staff would be required to maintain careful lesson plans and to be observed against the 'common approach' criteria agreed on the training day at the start of term.

The LEA director visited on the last day before the half-term holiday and met with the head and deputies. Mr Moore found there was 'no need for my paper or a nuclear device ... because he agreed to all I wanted'. There was immediate agreement that the action plan should be reviewed to see whether the objectives could be achieved more cheaply; that the LEA would support Mr Moore's plan to re-structure the school's staffing; and that the LEA would check and verify the budget figures that had been presented and approve a deficit recovery plan, spread over several years if necessary.

Although the outcome was satisfactory, Mr Moore was surprised to find that the director was 'nervous of me' and worried that 'my two main objectives – survival and exit special measures – still seem a long way away'.

Pressure and support

David Brown, the geographer who believed he had 'lost my way' (see chapter 3) after the Ofsted inspection, was one of the first teachers called in for a personal development consultancy. When he broke down and described how Ofsted had undermined him, Mr Moore was sympathetic and in his diary questioned the wisdom of a harsh policy on poor performance. Some teachers had been undermined or driven to despair, while there were others who felt victimised for weaknesses in the school that were not of their mak-ing. Mr Moore agreed to support David through an extended men-toring programme, backed up by external training in geography methods. Elaine, the deputy head responsible for humanities, and herself a geography teacher, warned Mr Moore about David's track record:

> ...there was an awful lot of unpleasantness about the previous head of department ... he did support him a great deal in ways that he either didn't see, or refused to see or couldn't see ... you have got a very complicated individual there who plays different games de-pending on what mood he's in or how he sees things.

Mr Moore also compared notes with Jenny, the recently arrived head of humanities. She explained that her brief had been to sort out the department, including David:

Mr Goodlad told me the department had two exceptionally talented teachers and two teachers who struggled and your job is to have two struggling teachers come to some sort of acceptable standard. So if these two people had difficulties, obviously one prong was the external training but what my priority had to be was to raise their awareness of how to deliver quality teaching and learning.

David Brown had buttonholed Jenny on her first day at Hillside:

...he more or less told me his history of involvement at Hillside. His history with the head, the past head of department and the history of his back illness and his experience of Ofsted and more or less told me he was hoping for better things from me ... I had in the back of my mind that he had something specifically wrong with him that he wanted me to know about.

Jenny described the version David had given her of his disastrous Ofsted lesson:

...he was standing in the room and things were going on around him and he had no power to control what was happening ... as if he was standing in a tunnel really and the lesson was just going badly wrong in front of him with the inspector sitting there ... there was far more to it than somebody numbed by the fear of being in-spected.

Mr Moore was positive about the first of David's lessons he observed. There were 'only seventeen in the room and hands up all the time'. The walls were decorated with maps, children's work, and pictures from around the world. Mr Moore thought the lesson was 'highly organised' and afterwards enjoyed leading David through the self-evaluation *pro forma*. Although he was 'on the whole ... impressed', he explained to David that 'while the lesson is complex with lots of variety ... his teaching was itself one-paced'.

On his next visit three weeks later, Mr Moore was less pleased. David had 'struggled to string a lesson together out of a couple of test sheets and a map ... his pace was slow, his responsiveness to the pupils poor'. When he consulted with the head of humanities, Jenny questioned how long the school could tolerate David 'switching children off and generating incidents'. She had recently observed a lesson herself where there had been little interaction between David and the class. The number of disciplinary incidents was increasing and David was sending students straight to Jenny. She felt it was the strategy of 'a passive aggressive, who is complaining and trying to dump things on your doorstep'.

Elaine reported a steady flow of complaints from the children:

> ...a lot of kids don't relate to him particularly well and complain about him. They complain in social terms that they don't like him as an individual and some have complained ... because they don't feel they get anywhere.

She identified a common thread running through their cases of poor teaching:

> ...look what we've dealt with so far this year. All those people who are dealing with things poorly in the classroom. I hesitate to use the word bonkers, but that's what we're looking at aren't we?

During an evaluation of a lesson, Mr Moore challenged David's failure to make the learning objective clear. The teacher was at first 'tough and depressed ... then soft' and finally conceded: 'It looks as though it's back to the drawing board for me, I thought I was making progress.'

David complained to Peter, the pastoral deputy, about the head's attitude during this interview. Meanwhile, Mr Moore recorded his belief that: 'David is hopeless and would be kicked to pieces by normal size classes.' He was like a 'lead weight ... dragging Jenny down and she's weary of it'. As capability proceedings now seemed inevitable, Mr Moore decided to disengage from his support role. He arranged for Peter to take over responsibility for the mentoring programme.

After Christmas, Mr Moore had to deal with a sequence of complaints and incidents involving David. Two girls objected to being separated from one another in geography. The head mediated between them and their teacher, listening to both sides of the story before inviting them to meet with him over lunch. Eventually one of the girls conceded that she had worked better since being made to sit on her own. At a parents' evening one father asked whether his son could give up geography because he was making so little progress. Mr Moore reassured him that the 'lessons are competent and contain all a serious individual would need to achieve the desired result.' This reassurance was unexpectedly endorsed by HMI during their first monitoring visit in January. Mr Moore noted in his diary: 'David is praised for a lesson, which sends him home deliriously happy. When I mention all the work on David but indicate my worries they refer to his 'good' lesson.'

Within a few weeks, David was reported to be suffering from depression. Mr Moore believed that the number of incidents with children 'have increased in volume as David's personal problems have increased. He's attending therapy and the children are treated with impatience and lack of consideration.' In the space of a single week, David was involved in an unseemly scuffle with a girl who refused to hand-over her personal stereo; slapped a boy round the back of the head 'to get his attention'; and dragged another girl to the front of the class where he insisted that she explain the difference between a stalactite and stalagmite.

Mr Moore thought that schools like Hillside were prone to collect 'vulnerable individuals', while Jenny believed that inspection was often the trigger for nervous collapse, touching the 'genie' people carried around with them: 'Whatever it was, Ofsted touched the button and I could predict how people would react, who'd break down.' Both considered that something had to be done, despite David's delicate and unpredictable state of mind. As Jenny later remarked:

> It's like a student in a class whose emotional and behavioural problems are such that they take up a lot of teacher time. You have to judge how far your strategies are helping that child and how far they affect the rest of the class.

Mr Moore wanted his moves 'to have an element of surprise' but worried there was 'a risk of tipping David over the edge.' An outside adviser warned him to be careful and suggested that David would either go sick or call in his union.

When he eventually met with David, the meeting was highly charged. David denied physical contact with the children. Mr Moore asked him to consider whether his own attitude was contributing to some of the problems that were occurring. The meeting was interrupted before progress could be made and David was then absent for six weeks with stress-related illness. When he returned to work, Mr Moore set up a lunchtime meeting to continue the conversation. The aim was to persuade David to adopt a more conciliatory approach to his students.

When Jenny challenged his mismanagement of the GCSE coursework a month later, David burst into tears and was so distressed that Peter had to take him home. Jenny thought his sudden collapse was because 'as the exams approached I think he panicked more that he hadn't done as much preparation as he might have'. Mr Moore believed that David had already 'half destroyed himself without my raising a finger' and hoped the problem was resolved when a sick note arrived to cover the next month:

> He is the fifth long term absentee. On paper he's a victim of Ofsted; of Moore; of Hillside. I don't now buy it. He's a profoundly unhappy man who has great difficulties sustaining relationships with children and adults. His self-esteem problem leads him into endless misery.

To everyone's surprise, however, David rang Jenny about returning to work. He was unsure whether he could cope with Mr Moore's demands. According to Jenny, Mr Moore:

> ...had come to be the person he projected all ill on to. You were then denounced ... as the person putting on too much pressure. My personal opinion is that you are only expecting him to be professionally responsible.

But David was also dissatisfied with the help he had received from Jenny as head of humanities:

> He said to me many times that I haven't helped because comparing himself to me, I am a very, very different teacher and that hasn't helped him.

Determined that David should not return to school for a few days then disappear again, Mr Moore insisted on meeting with him before he resumed classroom duties. As far as the head was concerned, 'it is important to clear up his allegations about my supposed 'pressure'. Incidents will occur and I do not intend to be blocked by fear of his accusation.' David agreed to the meeting without demur and told the head that he was very much better. His doctor had advised him 'not to give up taking the tablets, he believes the problems may well be chemically induced'. He insisted that he no longer had dark dreams in which the head appeared 'as a demon'.

Elaine believed that David was a 'lost cause':

> If you are particularly tangled and particularly complex and you're having difficulty in seeing where other people are coming from and see how where you are coming from is seen by them, you know all the perceptions are all mixed up, then you're never really going to get very far ... the best teachers are those who've got a fairly clear vision about what they're doing, a clear vision about how it's perceived and can handle that.

David continued to teach at Hillside for two more years.

Leadership: impact and response

At first, Mr Moore startled the teachers and students at Hillside. Stephen was among those who were suspicious after their recent ordeal:

> We have had three heads in such a short time. What has Mr Moore come in here to do? It might be quite innocent – to get on with the job; or has he been given another brief? We don't know. I might get on fine with him, but you have got to ask that – you just don't know the answer.

Elaine sensed that: 'A lot of trust is being withheld and people are approaching everybody now with caution because they are not quite sure what is going on ... I don't know if they know quite exactly how much they can trust us any more.' She also pointed to a sharp difference in style between Mr Goodlad and Mr Moore:

> Mr Moore is bigger words and longer sentences and he is that bit more academic in his approach to the kids than Mr Goodlad was. Mr Moore seems a little more remote from the kids and he doesn't have that kind of empathy with them but he has a procession of kids to his door to talk to him.

But people were soon responding to his positive attitude. The caretaker said: 'Mr. Moore's got the personality and he is a wonderful person ... smiling, approachable, follows things ... and you feel you have got his support.' Stephen was pleased with a note of thanks saying that he had done 'a grand job' with work experience: 'I have never ever been told that before ... it is little things like that goes a long way – someone has noticed me! ... Mr Wake, he did nothing, not a thing.' Jean said that colleagues began to value his 'open door policy to staff and students', while Jenny noticed that senior management were now 'very quick to praise, verbally and in writing' and was 'impressed by the regard in which I feel held. I certainly feel an equal.' Darren felt that younger teachers 'don't feel reluctant to speak now ... you can see Mr Moore taking on board the information but saying well yes but...'

Jean thought students were initially a bit wary of Mr Moore, 'because his predecessor was so good' but by the end of his first autumn term they were warming to him because 'he is seen as a firm headteacher who is consistent ... and fair.' Anne noticed that: 'If a child complains about a teacher ... he always likes to get right to the bottom of an issue.' Jean reported that students also liked his sociability, for example:

> ...the way he was willing to get up on stage and dance during the Diwali evening ... it helped bring a human quality, that you don't have to be stuffy if you are a headteacher.

Elaine described the change in attitudes:

> I think they quite like him but ... they are taking their time to make their minds up ... he has a sort of intellectual remoteness about him ... but they find him perfectly approachable.

Clive thought Chris Moore wanted to 'shift the culture from blaming staff to a supportive, collaborative one'. The caretaker commented that Mr Moore had 'introduced all this hard work. He's the first one here in the mornings and the last one to go so it just shows, you know, how hard he works and obviously wants everybody else to follow.' Stephen saw that Mr Moore 'has got a lot of enthusiasm, a lot of drive, seems to exist to work.' Anne remarked that he 'expected an awful lot of staff.' He produced 'loads of paper-work and sets up loads of meetings.' Clive saw him as:

> ...absolutely relentless ... does not tolerate mediocrity and he's clear to people ... but he is also prepared to go very softly until the point where he feels that there is no more capacity in that person to deliver.

According to Elaine, everything was 'much more clearly defined than it was before', especially in terms of line management. He inspected the school before public events occurred and, to the dismay of colleagues who had worked hard on their displays, picked out 'some old stuff' for critical attention.

As PAG chair, Clive realised that Mr Moore would be useful in the campaign ahead. He described the new head as:

> ...energetic with a strong intellect ... knows how to carry things through, honest but a political operator – a strategist who is clear about where he can put his energies, knows how to get on board influential people.

Clive also thought that parents were pleased with Mr Moore's arrival:

> The parents admire him. That level of positive regard ... is quite an important feature of running a school. On key occasions he's at community events and presents sharply and well. People are slightly in awe of him, but that is not unhelpful. I think people who have actually needed to speak to him have found him very approachable and warm, so that's OK.

> [The parents knew that] a minor revolution has been brought about ... young people in the school have spoken to visitors ... in glowing terms ... They have been talking with pride ... about their team. There is a strengthened sense of identity with the school, a sense of belonging.

Mr Moore concluded his diary for the first half of term with the words: 'Goodness, I've worked hard.'

5

Dictatorial Powers

Kitchen cabinet

After the half-term holiday, advertisements were drafted and placed for the business manager and office manager posts created by the support staff review. Mr Moore found it strange to be 'working on this now, weeks after the review' and told himself that it was nonsense to believe you could 'turn a school round in a week, fortnight, term'. As Gerald, the old bursar, was out of action and neither of the vacancies could be filled before January, there was quite a problem keeping the administration going. Fortunately the review also confirmed and extended the role of head's personal assistant, established informally by Brian Goodlad, so there were immediate benefits. Anne showed that she was prepared to work hard for a high quality result and became a member of the informal inner cabinet, acting as chief of staff to the head and two deputies and managing Hillside's personnel administration.

Like Elaine and Peter, Anne had been a junior member of staff before Mr Goodlad arrived. Under Mr Moore, she extended her scope to manage a constant flow of business, including appointments, correspondence and documentation for the governor and staff committees and working parties that began to flourish during the autumn, as well as the paperwork for senior management, Ofsted and the PAG. She co-ordinated and advised the chair of governors, the clerk to the governors, the PAG chair and many other official and unofficial visitors to the school. Mr Moore considered that 'her common sense, ability to anticipate problems and read situations makes her more like a deputy than a secretary'. She alerted Mr Moore to hazards ahead, informing him about unhelpful staff and shifts of opinion within the school and community. Although she was not herself perceived to be involved in manoeuvring for position, she was an indispensable part of the information network and ensured that new systems and procedures became operational. Peter thought the school would stop running without her. Mr Moore realised that he had become dependent on his kitchen cabinet and was consciously organising his workload around it.

Elaine and Peter both proved satisfactory. He thought Elaine's work on the curriculum was brilliant. She managed the group well and produced a series of closely reasoned broadsheets with all the implications and possibilities worked through. When he was tempted to interfere with Elaine's curriculum plan he saw that she was 'very, very crestfallen' and he changed his mind, deciding to stick with his promise to implement whatever the staff working group proposed. In his diary he noted:

> ...it is not right now for me to come in and start second guessing and throwing up all these questions ... I apologised and she was thoroughly relieved.

Peter led the pastoral team very successfully. A year head commented: 'There's no hidden agenda, he does it for the good of the school'. Students and staff regarded him as 'hands on'. They recognised that he found it difficult to give up his direct involvement with the pastoral casework that had been his main responsibility as a year head six months earlier. Peter helped design the Access database to monitor progress and watched attendance, which he thought could easily slip before the next monitoring visit. With his tutoring and mentoring working group, he produced a stream of policies and procedures, including admissions, induction, attendance and punctuality, homework and mentoring.

Chris Moore also used the deputies to check his own impact. Elaine told him that 'everyone's tired and you mustn't overload them', advice he valued because he was uncomfortably aware of his tendency to be 'driven by the demands of the agenda, by action plans, by fear, by excitement and then transmit it to others'. Later he was reassured that the deputies 'have got used to my drive, they haven't asked me to slow down much in the last few months, even when I've double checked with them'. And he intervened to protect the deputies when they ran into troubles of their own. When a student complained that Elaine was missing lessons to work on management issues he was told: 'She's already racked with guilt, she doesn't need you to tell her!'

The formal senior management team was scheduled to meet once a week and soon became a much less congenial grouping. Julian was a senior teacher, responsible for modern languages and assessment. He greatly regretted his decision not to take early retirement at the same time as Mr Wake and the others who had departed before Brian Goodlad arrived the previous March. Unhappy with the new head's insistence on long meetings and overcrowded agendas, Julian protested. Mr Moore recorded the incident in his diary:

> SMT began with Julian declaring that he would be leaving at 4.30 come what may and complaining about the length of Monday's staff meeting and about the content, which he felt was unjustified. He didn't allow me to laugh it off, repeated his determination to go and wanted to know what I would do about it. 'Get the governors on to me?' I responded pretty angrily and did not succeed in hiding my annoyance.

The meeting became 'intensely uncomfortable'. The others present were startled and embarrassed by the strength of the head's reaction. But he felt there was no alternative:

> Julian speaks with authority, wisdom and conviction but I am quite clear he can't have it his way. It is because nobody met to discuss anything that the school got into its difficulties but he grew up with, was happy under, and doesn't see the problems with, the old regime. He is a survivor, trapped on a journey he's fed up with by the new pension rules.

Chris Moore told Julian he had 'no hope of understanding, never mind contributing to, a discussion of the curriculum scheme in 40 minutes' but Julian replied by telling the head to get on with the agenda. Afterwards, talking with Elaine, Mr Moore was upset, believing that he had mishandled Julian's truculence. Elaine was at pains to reassure him. 'Julian put you on the spot, that's Julian ... the overall picture is good.'

Mr Moore acknowledged that the particular combination of personalities in the senior group had produced '*de facto* two management teams' and described a typical meeting of the full SMT:

> SMT is a fair non-event, as it's set up to be. Sidney isn't trusted so people are cautious what they say; Julian's ready to go before it starts; Donna needs time to unwind before she'll talk easily; Graham worries about departmental issues ... the easiness of Elaine, Peter and I is lost in the confused agendas of those present.

The head and deputies formed a cohesive, closely co-ordinated inner cabinet that met several times a day to take decisions and work up policies that were then presented for comments at the weekly full SMT. Sidney and Julian would offer opinions and occasionally introduce issues of their own. Mr Moore regarded these as potentially dangerous. Julian, for example, persisted with his demand that the school's time budget be re-calculated, knowing that the extra meetings introduced by the new head had overloaded the 1265 hours specified in the School Teachers' Pay and Conditions document. Mr Moore responded by asking Elaine to lead a working group, including union representatives, to complete a full review by the end of the academic year.

He did not trust senior management to deliver what he wanted and manoeuvred around the group of people brought together by Mr Goodlad, frustrated because he said he wanted 'dictatorial powers to deal with problems' while some of his colleagues wanted to 'carry on in the same comfortable old way.'

Disappeared without address

As the individual interviews continued, the new head began a series of classroom tours to improve his knowledge of the teaching at Hillside and embarked on a round of lunches with departmental staff to discuss improvement. At first he was unsure what to make of the lessons he saw:

> I wander round the school twice, visiting most classrooms. Di's poor relations with students were evident, she seems to have no

'knack', her responses seem naturally brittle and too much. There are others where the teachers teach sitting down. Ian is in his chair as if he were on the bridge of the Enterprise. Everywhere there are rows and writing. But the behaviour is good. The whole atmosphere, from my perspective, remains unnatural, with small classes, passive teaching strategies and lots of empty space.

He considered several lessons to be unequivocally poor, however:

William doesn't explain or introduce or summarise or round up. He just ploughs into abstract activities the children don't really like or understand and talks over the top of everyone until the time runs out, providing a negative, discouraging commentary on everything he can think of. The tasks are straight from the book.

He wondered how to debrief the teacher without being negative but was surprised when William admitted the lesson was 'crap' and agreed that he had not completed the required scheme of work either. Increasingly, as he coached David and encountered other colleagues with similar problems, Chris Moore recognised that he had to deal with 'nice, well-intentioned, intelligent, personally sad, almost tragic figures' but was clear that 'they are failing to perform the basics of the job'. The big question was how to sustain morale while dealing with such serious problems. Elaine told him to take the issues 'one at a time'.

In his diary the head recorded that one teacher 'disappeared without address for an indefinite period' and 'moved on to depression, divorce and homelessness'. The consultations also revealed that several colleagues were dreaming of retirement:

Why do conversations revert to retirement and opting out so often, even amongst those who are making little visible effort? Or perhaps it is an effort for them.

One long-serving teacher had calculated that 'compared with retirement, he is working for £300 per month', a thought no doubt prompted by the premature retirement of five colleagues the previous term. A young teacher, who had been made redundant from her previous school, had become ill in the immediate aftermath of the Ofsted inspection and by the end of term was unable to go on. She told the head that when she said she would come back to work she had felt good but that she had been anxious and worried ever since. She didn't mind the children but was overwhelmed by the other demands of the job, like marking course work, collecting absence notes, attending meetings and working at night.

Chris Moore asked himself whether she had been 'vulnerable in the first place, with shallow reserves of energy'. He concluded that she 'has a very wide range of skills but has been squeezed' so that even the least effort caused tiredness, sleeplessness and acute anxiety. Others seemed detached from reality and provoked complaints from their colleagues and students. A distressed group of children said they couldn't understand what one teacher wanted them to do and were upset that he insisted on silence when all they wanted was an explanation. Mr Moore began to investigate a complaint and was immediately frustrated by the teacher's response:

> He wants to argue about the meaning of words, the philosophy of language, the motives of others ... he's all over the place in an ordinary conversation, never mind a lesson.

On another occasion, Mr Moore checked out a teacher criticised in the inspection report and discovered 'an awful cacophony with no obvious teacher interventions or direction. What were they doing and why were they doing it?' In a neighbouring classroom, he found year eleven students 'doing nothing' and was embarrassed as the teacher told him that 'they can be quite difficult' and that they had been reluctant to read as directed. A more capable teacher saw himself as permanently tired and told Chris that he had 'learned not to be too energetic and lively because I got exhausted'.

The agenda for the departmental lunches was designed to be positive. Departments were asked to report their expected number of GCSE higher grades and to explain how they would contribute to the development plan and the reading improvement targets. The modern linguists used their lunch to protest. Julian told the head: 'We're duplicating here Chris, it's all in the scheme of work, we're wasting time writing things out, our teaching is ok, we're being punished for the failings of others.' The head's response was to 'read them the inspection report paragraphs on languages, which highlighted exactly the failings the planner is designed to correct'.

Other teachers were reluctant to change and failed to comply with Mr Moore's requirements for lesson planning and assessment. In his diary he noted that 'there are signs that people aren't too keen on the planner, on taking the register; hope to get by in much the same old way'. A temporary teacher said that his partner 'doesn't like him working in the evenings' while a head of department 'fills in the planner after the sessions as a record; the opposite of its purpose'. Mr Moore decided to take this 'evidence of resistance' as the text for 'a sermon' at morning briefing:

> ...gently reminding people of why we agreed to progress with a common planning framework and emphasising that it is not a voluntary activity. We've been caught out for lack of suitable structure, planning and monitoring and now have to be seen to have appropriate procedures.

There were flickers of ideological opposition as well as resistance to the increased demands of the job. One experienced and effective teacher 'dislikes the national curriculum' and informed Mr Moore that 'there has to be something outside teaching, there has to be time for family, I'm working all the time already'. A good teacher declined promotion because 'it would take up too much of my time'. William openly admitted 'that he hasn't done the schemes of work. He's had so much to do', and shrugged when told the task was an action plan priority. Across the corridor, another subject leader said he would like to be a restaurateur and intended to 'put family and health' first.

Senior management audit

Although he was still not sure whether he should have a personal role in monitoring lessons, Mr Moore used a staff meeting in early November to introduce his proposal that senior and middle managers should monitor lessons. He believed that with the audit and a planned 'mock monitoring' visit by the deputies, '...we shall fulfil the action plan's commitment to monitoring and evaluation in spades'.

Appraisal and monitoring systems were set up as part of a strategy to improve the consistency and quality of teaching, as required by the action plan. A senior manager was assigned to each department, with a monitoring role to include:

■   observing lessons

- discussing the development plan, including staffing, facilities, equipment, resources and training

- monitoring the use of the staff and student planners

- checking homework, marking, behaviour, discipline and the registration of students.

This ensured that the senior staff helped implement a potentially uncomfortable innovation, removed possible sources of opposition and emphasised the positive, developmental aspect of classroom observation. When HMI visited, the inspectors were presented with files of reports on every teacher, each compiled by a senior manager. Routine audits were supplemented by 'mock monitoring' designed to rehearse HMI visits. The head was concerned that although Hillside had been in special measures for over a year, there had been no contact or communication with Ofsted or with the Standards and Effectiveness Unit at the DfEE. He began to question whether there was such a thing as special measures.

At the end of November the deputies toured the school for two days and simulated the anticipated HMI procedure by unexpectedly entering classrooms, observing parts of lessons, checking behaviour and scrutinising lesson plans, exercise books and assessment records. After Christmas Mr Moore decided to join the monitoring team himself and challenged a number of staff about their unsatisfactory practice. When one teacher was summoned to explain the point of his lesson and why the children were drawing cartoons, he told Mr Moore that: 'he had been ill, that friends of his had died, that his relatives were seriously ill but that none of that was an excuse for what he accepted was, in fact, a disaster'. His department head also felt criticised and burst into tears while describing what had happened. The teacher's short-term contract was not renewed.

According to Mr Moore, 'mock monitoring' yielded 'an enormous volume of material for reflection and action' and supplied the senior team with detailed information about their colleagues' morale and performance. The audit process and subsequent questioning could be remorseless. One thing he asked about was a departmental handbook, which he criticised as 'an unusable, motley collection of scraps that won't help anyone teach'. Apparently reassured by the reply that updating the handbook was the next priority, he allowed time for progress to be made. But after further visits by the two deputies, Chris Moore summoned the member of staff to explain why he did not teach his class more actively. The department head complained that it was his 'second bollicking in two days'. The head warned that inspectors would be less than impressed to find rows of quiet children 'set little tasks out of the book'.

Rejects and pussies

Although his firm stance had won the support of the staff, Mr Moore found himself drawn into dealing personally with more and more difficult students, to the point where he felt like a social worker with an overwhelming caseload. Like Mr Wake and Mr Goodlad, Mr Moore found it 'harder and harder to fend off all the rejects from other schools who want to come here'. The specially contrived admission and induction arrangements regulated and delayed the arrival of new students but, as Peter told the head, parents were too persistent to be discouraged by procedural devices. Mr Moore was concerned about the cultural divide between Hillside and Brownville students and the disruptive potential of the dysfunctional young people who passed through his office:

> So you have got part of a school that is aspirational and quite middle class in what it wants to do and what it wants to be involved in and then you have got the sort of rump working-class Britain which goes along if you treat them right.

Problems with students were compounded by the high rate of staff absence and sickness. The head noted that the five teachers on the long-term sick-list had to be placed at the head of the cover list before routine illness and training were considered. This meant that for many students two lessons out of the six might possibly be taught by supply teachers, usually with poor results for discipline, behaviour and attitude. Although visitors noticed that 'the children are so gentle and pleasant compared with what might hit you in other local schools', and an LEA adviser used the phrase 'pussies' to describe the children's willingness to go along with teachers, Mr Moore found 'the number of off-the-wall disciplinary cases is pretty high, with some extreme, semi-hysterical behaviour'. Reluctant or ineffectual staff combined with the long tail of the school's intake to generate a time-consuming caseload of disciplinary incidents. The head reported that:

> The tally of incidents grows faster than we can deal with them and my diary is swiftly peppered with appointments with parents to disentangle frustration, anger and disaffection between teachers and children.

Mr Moore was scrupulous when he investigated complaints by students or staff. According to Anne, who arranged all his appointments:

> If a child complains about a teacher then he has to have the teacher in for a discussion to get their side of the story. Then he has to have the child back.

He tried to understand the points of view involved, to support the teacher, however much at fault, and to salvage everyone's honour. The aim was to defuse conflict that might prove disruptive and to coax staff and students back to the classroom for work. But as he recorded in his diary:

> You are dealing in human relationships, not crime. Each case is different, each requires sustained long term help, support and negotiation, each consumes infinite time.

Absentees, emotionally vulnerable individuals and weak practitioners diluted the positive impact of those teachers who were able to respond enthusiastically to the changed climate and initiated new extra-curricular activities, public celebrations and more varied teaching methods.

The head believed the school was 'very vulnerable to recycled children excluded from elsewhere', who would have been problematic however skilful the teaching. He expected trouble with an admission although the boy and his mother announced their keen interest in education. Another was accepted though he suffered from attention deficit syndrome. At his previous school he had climbed on the roof and given teachers the V-sign before being expelled for a violent attack on a fellow pupil. In the past, Mr Wake had been blamed for the admission of disaffected students, but Mr

Moore soon discovered that if there were vacant places it was hard to turn people away, however disruptive and dysfunctional they seemed at interview.

'Recycled' students were not the only ones who proved difficult. Some admitted in the ordinary way were equally troublesome and pursued agendas unconnected with GCSE results or achievement of any kind. Mr Moore felt that Katrina was 'intensely intelligent but self-destructive'. With her friend Tracey, she spent a good deal of time in the toilet between and sometimes during lessons. They would haunt corridors, get into scrapes with other students and endlessly gossip about the loves and hates of the girls in their class. Neither cared much about learning.

One student became a father and lost all interest in school. He disappeared, even though he was offered a part-time schooling package. Mr Moore met with a lone mother who was in despair:

> ...her boys often lose their tempers, kicking doors, walls etc. 'My ex was like that, I've holes in the wall to prove it,' she says. 'I wonder if Russ saw too much of him abusing me?'

When questioned about her threatening behaviour and bad language, a particularly volatile student told the head that her mother had just married a much younger man: 'I don't have a problem with school; I have a problem at home which I bring to school.'

Chris Moore's diary shows him to have been continually dealing with dysfunctional rather than disaffected students and families, meeting with adults, counselling children and calming staff. He found almost all the children 'open and friendly' and recognised that troubled families were no less concerned about their sons and daughters than those in more fortunate circumstances. Parents valued the efforts of pastoral and teaching staff to help their youngsters through personal and emotional problems. He worked to 'negotiate staff attitudes and expectations and avoid flare-ups with parents and children while doing so'. Sometimes he was close to despair, commenting that he had been 'sucked into an exhausting morass of student issues' and lost the 'thread of serious planning'. Even in the lunch queue, he had to stop a fight.

Disturbed home lives often led to irregular attendance. There were long-term absentees in each form by years ten and eleven, so that the small bottom sets became progressively smaller as the GCSE course progressed. A teacher reported that in year eleven 'about seven students decided long ago that French was not for them'. The head and his colleagues questioned the relevance of GCSE for many students who seemed to them at risk.

At one level Mr Moore was concerned with control and harmony; at another he felt a personal engagement with people in trouble. A boy and girl in year eight aggravated one another and were referred to the head:

> Both have experienced abusive families. Sarah is traumatised, clings to her mother; John erupts with anger when challenged and has already locked his mother in the bathroom. So I have the two round my table.

Mr Moore talked them into agreeing to support one another: 'You've both got problems, you both need support, couldn't you be friends?' John declared that 'I ain't doing nothing sloppy' but was incredulous when the head proposed a 'get to know you' bowling trip. In the weeks that followed, Mr Moore intervened repeatedly to remind them of their commitment to one another. But in the following term, Sarah fell out with a group of girls and her mother transferred her to another school.

No compulsory redundancies

An LEA finance officer brought surprising news that made nonsense of Mr Moore's earlier budget calculations. Although twenty per cent of the student roll had been lost, the Easton LMS formula did not require schools to repay funds that had been over-allocated the previous year, on the basis of estimated numbers. The officer presented the Hillside SMT with a draft budget that showed the special allowance for small schools increasing to offset the students that had departed. Mr Moore understood the implications at once:

> It means the budget gap could be half what we were working towards. We should be able to handle the reductions within the single year and without compulsory redundancies.

The overall position was about £100,000 better than expected. This discovery had a significant impact on the strategic review of the action plan that immediately followed. Mr Moore now believed the required reduction in costs could be achieved by discontinuing temporary contracts. He decided not to go for redundancies even if that meant risking a financial problem. Any attempt to preserve the redundancy option by issuing the relevant statutory notices would be very damaging and the potential saving would not be worth the pain. He was worried that he had misjudged 'the scale of the budget problem' but was relieved that the overall position was so much better than they had feared. And he was also more confident that the school could afford external appointments to the vacant business manager and office manager posts, which he saw as an essential step towards an efficient administration. Interviews were held and two suitable candidates were appointed.

Reassured on this front, the head and deputies pressed on with plans for new curriculum and staffing structures. One weekend Mr Moore prepared a draft staffing plan, which he handed to Elaine and Peter for comment. The aim was to produce a consistent, affordable structure with clear lines of responsibility and subject departments that were large enough for effective teamwork. He described his early morning meetings with Elaine and Peter as:

> ...my main influence route on the school, a vehicle and filter for ideas and progress chasing. They are invaluable, enabling us to monitor the work we're doing, to check progress, to bounce ideas off one another and to ensure calendar and timetable details.

Chris Moore acknowledged that 'I'm 90 per cent pressing forward during these meetings' but found that his deputies' 'judgement is invariably sound and they are a good test base for my initiatives'. They agreed to progress the review plan through the heads of department, the full staff meeting and the governors' strategy committee, as well as the full governors' meeting.

Mr Moore's influence was evident in Elaine's curriculum proposals, which she had succeeded in steering through her working group. Before Christmas there was no obvious dissent from the curriculum scheme as it passed through all the committees and meetings. By February, however, when the heads of department had assimilated the document, several began to oppose mixed ability grouping. Mr Moore intervened at once to amend the proposal and win their support without reopening the debate. He suggested that each department should have 'flexibility' with clusters of two or three forms:

> Science is resistant but quickly persuaded by my new formulation; Humanities is also won over. I convince them that it is wrong to give one department another's sets; and that the option of small bottom sets has all but disappeared ... English and Languages are won over.

As the head reported to the governors, when they received a much-amended document in the spring, Hillside would in future offer an entitlement curriculum, with a reduced number of options, more economic teaching groups, and flexible arrangements for subject setting.

Mr Moore regarded the stigma of the 'bottom set' as one of the school's fundamental problems and was determined to solve it:

> I think because of the bottom set mentality, we actually have designer misbehaviour here. We actually cause the problems that we then try to solve by repression. I am aiming to go out and win those kids for the school.

You're not going to shout at me are you?

The head continued to tour the school, 'to remind people I exist and to show I listen'. He mostly found supply teachers 'supervising people doing not very much'. He discovered that one of the English staff was off for the week with stress. Ian was 'supervising children fair-copying manuscript into the computers' and John was 'coaching a tiny maths class'. A biologist was 'teaching the characteristics of living things as delightfully as you could imagine'. At lunch he encountered a teacher who expected a rebuke:

> She said 'you're not going to shout at me are you?' and I said 'well, what have you done?' and she said 'well, I'm thinking of taking a sandwich out of the hall, will that be alright?'

The exchange reminded him of his earlier perception that: 'Mr Wake is now a scapegoat but I'll be living with his warped images for a long time to come.'

Like many staff, Mr Moore was worried about the behaviour of year ten and assembled them for a pep talk:

> Not a comfortable group of students at all, untidy in their seats and not very happy with what the school offers them. I embarked on a reasonable but firm path ... Pause to rocket late arrivals ... 'you hide in the toilets, don't do homework, don't bother with planners, disrupt teachers, interfere with other students ... it isn't satisfactory, you're shooting yourselves in the foot' ... and more in the same vein.

He suspected that the assembly was more for the benefit of himself and the staff than the students, who had heard it all before:

> As I spoke I was already thinking. We can't leave them like this for another two years ... why not remove a form, re-shuffle the students ... how about a residential experience? Is this because they lost a dozen brighter children during the implosion last summer?

He asked Peter and the new head of year to look at re-organising year ten and offered funds for adventure training courses at a local centre.

As the end of term finally arrived, with the main budget, curriculum and staffing issues resolved, at least in his own mind, Mr Moore attended the Christmas Extravaganza and reflected on the progress that had been made:

> Two hundred plus parents, staff and children all happily enjoying themselves, this time celebrating Christmas almost for the first time ... How far from their mood of last year, how far they've come, together. And they've done it themselves, through solidarity and determination ... This will do more for the quality of relationships and quality of learning than all the targets in the government book.

Technology

In early January the arrival of the new business and office managers and a phone call from HMI to arrange the first monitoring visit accelerated the pace of change. Mr Moore found the newcomers were: 'very positive and easily shocked by Hillside's lack of systems ... new financial systems are on their way ... the office manager is easily dismayed by the computers and routines'. Anne and Jeanne, the new office manager, worked together through the spring and summer to implement sweeping changes to the school's basic procedures. Improvements were made to:

- the postal and filing systems
- the management of student records
- the management information systems
- the reprographics service.

New systems were introduced to:

- enhance communications with parents and students
- streamline the management of exclusions
- professionalise personnel administration
- coordinate governor committees.

A Microsoft Access database was created to store and analyse student performance information. Efficiency gains were achieved in each case by introducing appropriate computer software to manage the new systems proposed by the head, deputies and other managers.

As Anne, Jeanne and the business manager laboured to establish straightforward, efficient systems and administrative procedures, Mr Moore felt he was 'riding with the tide on the administrative front' and rejoiced in 'the best administrative team I've had, three key, very able people with whom I talk more satisfactorily than the full senior management team'. With the administrative review proposals now in full operation, job descriptions linked everyone's work to the action plan, so that long-serving staff were also harnessed to new methods and objectives. He set up an administrative group to plan and monitor progress and soon began to worry that the business manager was already too powerful. He thought there was a risk that the deputies 'could find themselves marginalised by this burgeoning office outfit'. He advised Elaine to instruct the business manager to order the furniture she required. 'You'll need to win this one on your own, or he'll assume deputy heads only relate to children.'

Mr Moore began to observe lessons systematically himself, using the criteria from the approach agreed in September as a basis for discussion with teachers afterwards. He visited technology first, knowing that it was an area of weakness. Ofsted inspectors had commented that:

Low expectations and lack of pace also hinder pupils' standards and progress ... Curriculum leadership and management are weak.

The acting head of department, Stephen, felt the criticisms were unfair:

...the technology area needs a massive refurbishment and it is not within our budget ... I have been asking and asking just for new bench tops. I said I would make them – just give me the money for timber – 'no, can't afford it'. The management of design was criticised because the chappie was hardly ever here and senior management hadn't really responded to that, we should have had a supply teacher in who could take over the management of the department ... there were occasions when they were literally living from day to day.

Mr Moore observed George, who had taught at Hillside for over twenty years, guide fifteen year eleven students through their GCSE coursework. The lesson transcript was completed immediately following the observation and was included amongst the papers later submitted to the inspectors:

George calls the register and stands to one side (the room opens in various directions – to the forge, the machines, store area etc) to explain the mark scheme and assessment objectives for GCSE coursework. He offers the students extra time at lunch time to complete projects or move them forward. 'I want you cracking on with these ... I'll let people go to the library or to the computer room.' He draws attention to a spiral bound guide book which spells out what they have to do to make a success of their project. George sits at his desk and calls students up one by one for a consultation.

Three girls leave for the library when prompted. There are prompts on the board: 'Research, Analysis, Specification, Brief, Generation of Ideas.' One student asks for magazines. George directs him 'round the corner.' George then works through the register checking progress and offering pointers...

Work is at an early stage and the quality is indifferent without being scrappy. The pace is very relaxed, nobody attacking the task with urgency. George comments on one lad's productivity: 'You've taken 4 hours on that ... you need to get stuck in ... that should go with research ... presentation isn't bad at all.' He explains a point to Darren, making encouraging noises...

Students work quietly. George returns to his desk. Another student goes up. 'Put down where you've got that from. You've spent 4 hours of your time, are these all there is ... that is smashing that, if every sheet looked like that, smashing, brilliant.'

'You'll have to find out what other people think ... you've got to make sure the project can be produced in quantity ... the specification has to be right ... all I'm putting is I've looked at ideas, there are some nice ideas, but you need more, next lesson ... more.'

George calls for the attention of the class. 'If I've not looked at your work today, next lesson I'll certainly get round ... OK, begin to put things away.' Three minutes before the end most students have their coats on. Simon is chatting amiably with various others. George asks: 'Anyone else want an appointment for parents' evening?'

Pens are put away, everyone is packing up. Simon has wandered to several more groups but the atmosphere remains calm. 'Pencils still floating around chaps,' says George as clearing up proceeds quietly. As the bell rings the students dismiss themselves. 'Off you go,' calls out George after them, from his seated position at his desk.

Mr Moore doubted whether the extended time given to GCSE coursework was appropriate for less able students. Could 'they cope with no reward for so long?' Once the students had embarked on projects there was little that the teacher could do, 'beyond repeating simple advice or guidance and despairing because the candidates don't read or follow the instructions they've been given'. Thinking ahead to the HMI monitoring visit, the head wondered how inspectors would measure a lesson of this type. He almost sympathised with 'poor old HMI who have to observe and report on standards in one indifferent school and classroom after another'.

A consultant, hired to help the science department, presented an unsettling report. Although HMI were poised to visit, there was little evidence of regular homework, 'marking is not really done regularly', and there was widespread 'indiscipline and absenteeism in years ten and eleven, especially in the bottom sets'. The head told his deputies and the LEA inspector to have modest expectations of the first monitoring visit:

...we had a long way to go ... it would take time to deal with the poor teaching and establish new systems and cultures. Until the new timetable and curriculum have worked through, all the changes will be superficial and their impact will be on the surface.

At their regular morning meeting, the head and deputies worried about staff morale. What should be done to reassure their colleagues in the run up to the publication of the secondary review proposals in a month or so? They sensed 'three main levels of staff anxiety':

(a) Will I keep my points? (b) Will I have a job at the end of the year? (c) Will I have a job if the school is reorganised or merged? Better ... to let people know where they stand, give them a chance to find another job; even if some are unhappy, reassure the 90 per cent ... The problem is that people have been living in a world with a guillotine that doesn't drop for so long they no longer believe in cutting edges, only the fear of cutting edges.

At morning briefings, the head constantly reminded the staff 'to stick to the game plan' and insisted that 'our routine' in the classroom 'isn't an option and that people should stick to it because HMI will be looking for consistency.' As a final preparation for HMI, the deputies presented their report on the 'mini inspection' held before the holiday. They asked teachers to concentrate on the main issues that had been identified:

Disruption at start of lessons by latecomers; Lesson outcomes clear to all, perhaps on board at start of lesson? Disruption on the corridors and stairs. This includes students out of lessons and student movement around school between lessons; Reinforcing the usefulness of student planners; differentiation – use of/evidence of individual education plans being used.

Elaine and Peter also offered some encouragement, estimating that the proportion of lessons that were satisfactory or better had risen from 66 per cent at the time of the Ofsted inspection to 83 per cent at the time of their joint tour.

A couple of ferrets in your trousers
When two HMI arrived at the end of January they were presented with the head's Action Plan Progress Report, where he detailed the difficulties he had faced on appointment:

> Support and administrative arrangements were in disarray, with one secretary assigned to the general office ... The college's finances were almost inoperable ... no senior manager was assigned responsibility for financial management ... SIMS expertise was minimal. It was October before a reliable, SIMS-based pupil roll was established. A new telephone switchboard was promised for June ... but had not been ordered by September ... The lunch supervision scheme ... had not been established ... There are significant problems with the management of the (X) department ... which make it unlikely that the specified targets will be achieved ... Some departments were slow to develop schemes of work to match the analysis and consultants were employed to help them.

Chris Moore felt he had to 'confess to certain things to bank the necessary credibility but you can talk yourself into trouble by unnecessary frankness'. He also expressed concern about the impact on teachers in their classrooms:

> It's like having a couple of ferrets in your trousers. They go through everything, they inspect everything, they question everything, they move at incredible speed – I mean, they're very, very skilful I would have to say ... 30 lessons in a day.

He feared that 'even in positive inspections there is a huge psychological build up then deflation afterwards ... whatever your views on accountability, the actual physical process of a couple of blokes coming in and going through the drawers in your room and opening up your mark book ... is bullying.'

Despite his empathy with his colleagues, Mr Moore had presented special measures as an escape route from purgatory, a hard, narrow road to professional self-respect and survival. For months he had adopted the role of mentor and coach, as Jenny reported from her experience in humanities: 'He helped staff to have a particular structure to their lessons and also all teachers to have a lesson planning booklet.' Many teachers had responded to the opportunity to improve. Anne noticed that: 'One in particular has taken criticism very well. She wants to be better, which is lovely.' Anne was also impressed that Mr Moore dealt with 'those people who are not up to scratch' by explaining 'firmly, not bawling them out'.

Others were less clear about the benefits of the new approach and their fears mirrored the head's own reservations about the scrutiny to which they were subject. Clive believed that 'although Mr Moore has given a lot of support to weaker staff it hasn't necessarily been felt to be supportive. It has been felt to be scrutinising'. He argued that the Ofsted report and HMI monitoring visits had placed the head:

> ...in a very powerful position as a manager because he was not tainted with what went on before he came. The head uses Ofsted to mercilessly bring about change. The fact that it encourages a sense of blame and guilt should not hide the benefits that it brings. What remains to be seen is whether the changes are lasting.

Chris Moore accepted the truth of comments like these. He feared that his close monitoring and control of teaching would contribute to the 'intrinsic oppressive qualities' he detected in schools, hospitals and prisons. He was aware that his behaviour as head was 'driven by the demands of the agenda.' It was a dilemma beyond resolution, even in his diary:

> My attempts at rescue (myself, them) depends on ... (a) my will to power ... (b) the principles of comprehensive education ... learn from need and expression, not handed down, watered down, instructed ... (c) glass bead game with the oppressor (Bergman film, chess with death) ... but to win I must abandon (b). (a) and (b) mutually destructive – paradox of my career.

Other witnesses concentrated on Ofsted's destructive potential. Anne felt: 'Special measures is just too much. Everyone looks like zombies. I think they've had enough. Widespread depression ... they can still see a bit of a long haul ahead of them.' A long serving member of staff reflected that: 'people perform well under pressure for so long, then they're destroyed by it.' To others it seemed as if teachers 'are to be crucified ... for not converting a penny-pinched pre-fab into a Georgian country mansion.' As a governor, Clive sensed there was no longer any room for people who can't teach very well. But there was also a reluctant recognition that this was not altogether bad news. Anne said: 'I think all the other teachers realise that the ones who are being squeezed out are weak anyway and we do need some new young blood.'

At the end of their two-day visit, HMI reported:

> Teaching was satisfactory or better in three-quarters of lessons seen. It was good in a quarter but was also unsatisfactory in a quarter ... The marking and routine assessment of pupils' work is inordinately variable in quality ... Homework ... is not set sufficiently regularly and when it is set, the tasks are not always appropriate or worthwhile ... The headteacher, supported by the senior management team, provides strong leadership and a clear sense of direction. Teachers are responding to the high expectations he sets. Staff morale is steadying and generally improving ... The number of exclusions in the last term is already twice the national average *per annum.* This is not yet cause for concern, with a new headteacher wishing to establish clear rules, but requires close supervision.

Attendance had improved, averaging 89 per cent in the year so far, while 'every single indicator is up'. The school had made satisfactory progress with two key issues and good progress with the other two. Mr Moore felt that HMI had 'put together a picture of the school that to me was remarkably accurate and reasonable' and he admitted that 'HMI monitoring reinforced my picture'. His mind was 'immediately seething with ideas ... I want to start immediately. How can we sustain the pace?'

SWOT

The head's positive outlook changed briefly when he was told that a teacher had broken down after HMI had visited his classroom:

> ...the pain and pressure are endless. What next? My restructuring? Amalgamation? Another monitoring visit? And another? ... Then redundancy ... Imagine an end to failure, says Michael Barber in the *Dark Side of the Moon.* What about imagining an end to the torture? Or even to the uncertainty?

He was nevertheless excited by what he had learned from the visit. He had observed the two inspectors closely and believed he now understood their methodology well enough to orchestrate Hillside's exit from special measures:

> What we need for a couple of days in late May or June is evidence of progress. Not progress itself, but evidence. Documents, statistics, lessons which match the requirements. And thanks to the visit, I've mastered the genre. What we need is to gear everyone up for a perfect fortnight.

He called a staff meeting for early February and asked his colleagues to consider the school's strengths, weaknesses, opportunities and threats. Although the LEA budget was far better than expected and the HMI report was very positive, current levels of illness and stress were high. The revision of the schemes of work through the summer and autumn would greatly enhance consistency, while the proposed timetable and curriculum changes would make Hillside a coherent, efficient unit. The biggest threat was the secondary review that might lead to closure, demoralisation and redeployment next year. Mr Moore was certain that the new curriculum framework going into place for September would remove the small groups and create a more normal teaching environment for the autumn but was less confident about his ability to generate and demonstrate enough progress for the next monitoring visit, expected in June.

The pressure seemed intense:

> There's the staff structure to implement by April; the curriculum to become a timetable; the budget to finalise; the new development plan to write; all those policies and monitoring schemes to put in place. And above all, my burst of energy to produce the perfect two days for the inspectors has only half-materialised and there's precious little time now before Easter to complete all the preparatory tasks.

Chris Moore created the Access database. He envisaged a computer floppy disk containing performance data for every member of staff and set up a switchboard of enquiries that could be operated by staff whether or not they understand the software. At a specially convened meeting, he explained the revised staff structure and was greeted by silence, except from the head of sociology who thanked him the next day because it was the first time that anyone had tried to create some kind of rationale or system. The head and deputies worked on a development plan to replace the action plan, now complete apart from the commitment to continuous monitoring of the key statistics. He was surprised at the GCSE evening to find 'no anxiety expressed, no sense of impending withdrawals', despite the possibility that the school could be closed by the review. The parents seemed to accept the school's 'affirmation of our own continued existence'. A heads of department meeting was planned at a local hotel, where they would prepare for the June monitoring visit.

Mr Moore intended to leave nothing to chance or individual foibles and fancies.

In the midst of these plans and preparations, Mr Moore did not at first attend to the details of an incident in technology, where a student was alleged to have assaulted a member of staff. But on the day of the disciplinary hearing he discovered that the groundwork for the case had not been done and all the staff involved had other engagements. As he noted in his diary: 'So by evening I was obliged to present poor documentation about a girl I've never met.' The ensuing crisis nearly caused Chris Moore to resign.

6

Saved and Out!

Stabbed?

Chris Moore compared his approach to discipline with that adopted by Michael Duane, the Rising Hill headteacher whose anti-corporal punishment stance appears to have contributed to the school's troubles and eventual closure by the Inner London Education Authority (Berg, 1968): 'Duane seems to have regarded authority as objectionable in itself; I regard the effective use of authority as the problem.' Mr Moore's own use of authority was tested when a teacher was assaulted by a student shortly after the first HMI monitoring visit and in the lead up to the publication of the LEA's secondary review proposals.

Mr Moore had established formal procedures to manage incidents of this kind. Dismayed by the lack of system before his arrival, he had hoped to strengthen the governing body by improving its conduct of business: 'The [former] head just got rid of people. The governors didn't have a role and that's what was severely criticised in Ofsted.' As Clive acknowledged: 'Mr Moore has completely changed the culture of the governing body in terms of its procedures. There were no procedures before.'

A student support committee had been established and was required to deal with disciplinary issues and to provide disciplinary panels to deal with exclusion and permanent exclusion. The heads of year were expected to prepare and present evidence. The clerk organised hearings and prepared minutes and correspondence. The head therefore excluded the assailant, requested a disciplinary hearing before the governors and recommended permanent exclusion. He was confident that governors would endorse his decision, particularly as witnesses alleged that a knife had been used, though without inflicting serious injury.

Although the systems were established on paper, the governors and the pastoral tutors were inexperienced in handling disciplinary cases. Under the old head, year heads were never asked to present evidence at disciplinary hearings. According to Mr Moore: 'the governors need coaching into their role, the staff coaching into their role, the support staff need coaching into their role.' The inexperienced head of year 'didn't put a report together until the day of the hearing so that was thin and I was left ... with a very weak case about a really high profile and important incident'. The year head and another teacher who had investigated the assault were unable to attend the hearing, so Mr Moore had to present the case himself.

Now chair of the disciplinary panel, Clive had been concerned for some time about the growing number of fixed term and permanent exclusions brought before the governors:

> I worry for the child being excluded when the addition of mis-behaviour was made up of items with the same staff always being involved in incidents.

He wished to introduce greater rigour to the proceedings because:

> Those governors engaged in the student support committee seem to be in and out all the time because there's been a rush of ex-clusions over this last term. Far too many – several governors have been very concerned to ensure that they get very close to that pro-cess to make sure it is not being abused.

Although Peter, who was in charge of pastoral care, saw the assault as an 'open and shut permanent exclusion case', the governors were not convinced. Clive led the questioning of the head and discovered that he lacked first hand knowledge of the student or the incident he described to justify the permanent exclusion. Clive suggested:

...it could show that there are some teachers who do not know how to deal with awkward pupils ... he sees a situation ... where there has been a relationship breakdown with that teacher.

Another committee member commented that '...no teacher should be subject to assault, but there is a lack of depth of detail relating to this incident'. Clive asked the head 'if he felt that any serious assault on a teacher should always lead to a permanent exclusion', to which Mr Moore replied that 'other cases would be dealt with on merit and evidence' but that 'when cases lead to untenable situations, pupils should not return to school'.

The head withdrew to allow the committee to deliberate and returned to learn their decision. The governors considered that the case against the student was based on a single incident. The minutes indicated that:

...they did not believe that a case had been established, to their satisfaction, to show that every other method of discipline management had been explored in this case. The pupil should be reinstated. Whilst recognising the difficulties that such a decision may cause, they would wish the school to use the time available to make every effort to bring about the circumstances for a successful re-admission.

The governors had effectively decided to re-instate the student unconditionally. When Mr Moore discussed the case with his deputies the next morning, 'the full awfulness of it sank in. It was now a huge political *imbroglio*.' Alert to the immediate danger, Mr Moore struggled to contain the damage:

The staff will be outraged – there's now a massive problem in terms of staff attitudes and reactions. It could blow up. We could be like The Ridings in a few days if the wrong responses surface.

The head telephoned the assaulted teacher, contacted the teacher governors and recounted the details of the hearing to his deputies and other influential members of staff. His strategy was 'to keep everybody in my confidence and to go to the next governors' meeting with huge umbrage about the reinstatement' and to brief the teacher governors to raise 'a whole series of serious issues.' The assaulted teacher was a member of the NAS/UWT. A few days after the hearing, a union official arrived at the school 'wanting to ballot the staff about not teaching X when X comes back'. As the governors had reinstated the assailant unconditionally, there was no mechanism for re-exclusion. Mr Moore feared that Hillside might be caught in an explosion of media interest in violent students, just as the secondary review was about to report on the school's future. For a few days the atmosphere was tense:

> Assaults on staff have a special emotional charge. Unless I lead the staff counter-attack my credibility with them will be nil; if I do lead the charge, I'll be at loggerheads with the panel and possibly the entire governing body.

Fortunately, the assaulted teacher and her immediate colleagues were not eager to be at the centre of a media storm and were equally anxious not to compromise the outcome of the secondary review. Mr Moore's decision to lead the protest about the governors' decision, although he knew the school's case had been poorly prepared and presented, produced the desired effect in the staff room. He noted that: 'There is strong support for my stand, indignation about the re-instatement and a unanimous letter of complaint to be tabled.'

Mr Moore was determined to reverse the governors' decision and to continue the assailant's exclusion. The head saw the chair of governors and threatened resignation; he also intrigued with the teacher governors and the deputies about how to play the staff letter at the full governors' meeting. One of the deputies visited the student's home and arranged a meeting between Mr Moore and the family. The student's reluctance to return to 'that school' and adamant denial that any violence had occurred enabled Mr Moore to find a solution. The chair of governors persuaded the disciplinary panel to meet with teacher representatives and after a long discussion it was agreed that conditions could be imposed on the assailant's return. Mr Moore and his deputies already knew that the student would refuse to apologise or promise to behave well in future.

Mr Moore's conclusion was that:

> Two or three key governors can have a hugely disproportionate power, if they are on board with you, you can muddle through. If they start to take independent positions, you can be in great difficulty very quickly.

The incident aroused strong emotions, becoming a protracted, painful and disruptive element in governor staff relations. Mr Moore realised that although the governors 'are willing to nod things through without question; they'll approve documents they've not seen or read', they could also introduce an agenda of their own. Clive had a different perspective on the case:

> The rush of exclusions in the last term has been brought about by a more assertive disciplinary code which is attempting to be clearer but in the absence of, I believe, a properly thought through whole school behaviour policy. Some staff would say this is long overdue.

However, the chair of governors was bewildered by the head's attitude and could not understand why he thought it was a resigning matter.

Secondary review

As the secondary review unfolded, Mr Moore began to appreciate the extent of the pressure on the authority to improve the lack-lustre performance of Easton Schools:

> ...the LEA is hyper-sensitive about all the schools in special measures, secondary and primary, they're desperately worried that they may lose control and the government may take them over. The review is driven by the desire to sort everything out.

His consciousness of behind-the-scenes menace was increased when a DfEE adviser visited Hillside to ask questions about the LEA. Mr Moore was unsure how to respond: 'I didn't know for sure how to handle him. Was he friend or spy?'

When he read in the local paper that the chair of education and senior officers had been summoned to the DfEE, he concluded that there were 'wide and powerful forces which we ignore at our peril'. In the absence of effective communication, heads, teachers and even LEA employees were feeding gossip and speculation into their interpretation of events. Rumours spread quickly, including scurrilous suggestions about the sexuality and personal lives of senior officials.

Mr Moore felt obliged to devote considerable time to boundary management. He pushed hard for support, inviting senior officers and councillors to the school, with mixed results. Although the director had promised support, he had failed to impress Mr Moore with his vision or capability.

The MP found time for another gathering of Hillside supporters, while the Mayor attended an evening contrived to emphasise the school's improved results. The chair of the Education Committee was too busy to meet the head. With the school poised on the brink of closure, Mr Moore listened carefully for news of the local authority's intentions and concentrated on the targets most likely to clinch a good report. His intention was:

> ...to hammer on with getting out of special measures as a morale counter-balance to the possible demoralisation that may come from the LEA's plan.

When Clive and the head debated whether or not to launch a public critique of the LEA's handling of the secondary review, Elaine was alarmed:

> I've seen Mr Wake brought down, the vote of no confidence and the rest, I don't want to go there again, just when we've got the school moving forward.

Mr Moore dropped the idea of an attack on the review process and was persuaded to wait for the publication of the official proposals at the end of February.

The *success d'estime* of the first HMI monitoring visit helped him persuade officers and elected members that Hillside was making good progress and he ensured that the letter from Ofsted was circulated widely. He met Clive regularly to monitor developments and:

> ...to interpret what we have heard. Is the school safe? Are they afraid of judicial review? Do they fear me or would they like to finish us? Are they after the schools with no political support? What kind of steer does the officer team have?

Managing relations with the LEA became an increasing challenge. Hillside had accelerated and according to Mr Moore needed to 'speed up the slow, plodding council red tape so that we get somewhere'. Under pressure itself, the LEA seemed unable to monitor or develop its own systems and organisation because it was preoccupied with a secondary review that consumed political energy and resources without earning the commitment of local teachers. Mr Moore was afraid that the LEA 'chaos' was undermining his work at the school. There was a grave risk that his new staffing structure, designed to give permanent posts to all his staff, would be overtaken by events. His new posts would last less than a year if Hillside were closed or reorganised. As the review deadlines approached, Mr Moore felt that: 'We do not control much of the agenda and I sense that next year will see power and decisions slip further from my grasp.' There would be melt-down if the school were closed or merged.

He also complained about the nervous energy and thinking time consumed by the prospect of imminent closure and observed that 'you can see how schools get knocked off their improvement course.' However, this did not happen, mainly because Mr Moore convinced himself and his colleagues that getting out of special measures was the key to survival. He was determined to 'get to May or June and the next monitoring visit and get another good report.'

Meanwhile he was active on the telephone, talking with other heads and guessing the right moment for an initiative that might make the difference between life and sudden death. Above all, he feared that Hillside would be merged with another school and lose control over its own destiny. He discovered that the DfEE adviser had become 'the power behind the plan, constantly in touch, constantly adding touches'. After an ambiguous call, during which the adviser asked whether he would like to be the head of a new school on the Hillside site, Mr Moore concluded that he knew 'almost exactly what was proposed', a full two weeks before the review proposals were due to be published. When he reported the news, he was surprised that Clive was 'not particularly pessimistic' about the outcome and was 'cooler and less inclined to respond to the emotions of the moment'.

Towards the end of February, the LEA director convened the Easton heads to tell them that nineteen out of twenty one secondary schools would be affected by the result of the review. Papers would be sent out to schools by courier the following week. Mr Moore was fearful that 'Hillside could be imploding within a few weeks, with students and staff bailing out and recruitment nearly impossible' and was confirmed in his belief that the best way to hold the school together would be to use 'HMI monitoring as a focus.' He told the staff: 'We can do ourselves a lot of good if we get ourselves out of special measures and I'm beginning to visualise a plan to do it.'

When the LEA review proposals were eventually released, there were two options for Hillside School. It could be closed and re-placed by a new school on the same site or the school could 'con-tinue in its present form but with a catchment area revised' to ex-pand the number on roll. Mr Moore and Clive seized the oppor-tunity presented by the second option almost immediately. To-gether they:

> ...came up with a plan based on what happened with the Hammer-smith school where they declared it closed and reopened it without actually going through the statutory process.

Their proposal was designed to build on option two and to appeal to LEA officers as they struggled with decisions about closing, ex-panding and reorganising different schools. Instead of being merged with another school, so that all the staff would have to reapply for their posts, Hillside would change its name voluntarily, appoint a new, permanent headteacher at the earliest possible date, and accept children from a wider catchment area. All the current staff would keep their jobs. Darren warmed to the fact that: 'Mr Moore and the governors have come up with another plan to change the nature of this school next December'.

The plan asked a fundamental question. In the case of Hillside, where rapid improvement was already taking place and was ap-proved by HMI, why impose an unnecessary, time-consuming statutory process? The Hammersmith precedent showed that it was possible to avoid almost a year of uncertainty, confusion and demoralisation. Adding Hillside to the list of closing schools would throw away what had been achieved already and add unnecessarily to the complexity of the LEA's reorganisation.

Governors approved the plan and convened their own public meet-ing to consult with parents and the community. Anne remembered that there were 'three half-page adverts in the local press and a massive mail shot to every pupil's home'. Over 150 people came to the meeting and endorsed the scheme. Mr Moore handed the DfEE adviser a copy of the proposal, 'hoping to slide it into their thinking' and was delighted to receive an immediate call from one of the assistant directors who thought the scheme was 'interesting'.

Option one or two?

The five-week consultation period and the fear that the LEA would choose the first option and close Hillside threatened to extend the planning blight caused by the review into the indefinite future. Darren noticed that 'older staff are particularly uncomfortable. They are looking at the possibility that they might have to find another job.' It was obvious that:

> Mr Moore is trying to reassure staff by being confident with us but he can't really guarantee anybody's job ... but he is just keeping up to date with all the developments. We are getting print outs and notes from meetings he has attended.

Mr Moore worried that his staffing structure might become 'just another phase of the temporary and interim arrangements which have afflicted my colleagues'. He concluded that his position was no different from Mr Goodlad's the previous summer. There was 'incipient demoralisation and an acute need to buy teachers into the project at this critical stage'. He resolved to 'push my deployment through ahead of the LEA's publication of final decisions'. Although these decisions were imminent, the LEA did not have the legal power to insist on temporary appointments or to prevent the governors implementing their own structure.

Rather than fill vacancies by interview, Mr Moore invited members of staff to write to the head expressing interest in 'up to three posts, indicating their order of preference'. A carefully drafted procedure would be followed so that permanent post holders at Hillside were guaranteed posts and allowances comparable to their present positions. Temporary post holders would be given consideration before jobs were advertised. He told the consultative group that 'we just want to keep them motivated, we don't want any beauty contests and disappointment.' Mr Moore devoted three days to interviewing all the teachers to resolve outstanding contractual issues because he was determined to provide as much security as he could. He published an agenda for the interviews, linking discussion of next year's contract with preparation for the next monitoring visit. The strategy and personnel committee of governors met a few days later to endorse the structure and the appointments that had been offered. Mr Moore was pleased that the

> ...final position is so much better than feared. We're set to lose three teachers when I expected to lose about seven; and we've taken out half a dozen points when I aimed initially for a reduction of about fifteen. Most of the loss has happened naturally. The process has been without rancour, bitterness or divisions ... better than everyone has been led to expect, not least by me.

Eleanor believed that most staff accepted that: 'Most of what's happened was sort of inevitable. Once the curriculum was put into place for next year, you have got to fit your staff to the curriculum.'

Mr Moore hurried on with the Access database because he was keen to present the inspectors with 'persuasive evidence of data analysis, targeting and monitoring, as indicated in the report'. He prepared a table to show that year seven had made convincing gains in reading ability. An average ten months improvement in reading age, after adjustment for chronological age, was recorded, while the target group gained a remarkable seventeen months. With Elaine, he worked on a format for departments to use when revising their schemes of work. At a local hotel the heads of department were trained to play their part in preparing for the next monitoring visit.

Mr Moore believed that by 'raising expectations, challenging people to do things', he had 'generated a lot of action'. He saw the staff 'becoming more pro-active, more professional, more convincing' though he thought some teachers remained 'moth-eaten and cobwebbed'. Over lunch Elaine told him off: 'You've only seen one review, this lot have seen two, they're knackered.'

When the Review of Secondary Education Report finally appeared, Hillside survived the axe. The LEA director recommended option two for Hillside:

> ...the principle of expanding existing schools is more appropriate than the new start proposal put forward for Hillside as part of the proposals for consultation, because of the compressed timetable for implementing the review.

Mr Moore found the committee report and scanned through for the recommendations:

> Where are the recommendations? I find them. We've done it! Done it! 'Anne! I think we've done it!' I give her a hug and feel tears in my eyes.

Elaine and Peter rushed out for bottles of sparkling wine and the staff celebrated their salvation. Anne captured the feelings of many:

> It is fantastic news that we are not closing. We stay here. We keep our jobs and we are an expanding school. Fantastic news from the picture that was painted just over a year ago.

She said that Mr Moore had congratulated everybody on their hard work but 'we realise there is an awful lot to do and a long way to go even now.' Later, when the head wondered aloud whether their plan had influenced the result, Clive reflected that: 'The politicians have taken the easy way out. They always do.'

By the early summer, Hillside's future was secure. Ahead lay the June HMI monitoring visit, the November re-inspection, the appointment of a permanent head to take over when Mr Moore's contract ended the following year, and expansion to accommodate students displaced by the closure of neighbouring schools. However, for many, the trauma seemed unending. As Anne remembered:

> But some teaching staff are becoming disillusioned. It has been going on for so long now. We've been in special measures sixteen months.

Improving teaching

With the school's future secure, Mr Moore was 'able to offer genuinely permanent positions' and moved to fill the vacancies that remained open after the internal consultation was completed. Two heads of major departments and five newly qualified teachers were recruited through national advertisements to contribute to new areas of the curriculum or to improve areas that had been covered temporarily, and often unsatisfactorily, through the crisis of the previous year. The head was excited at the prospect of newcomers arriving to reinforce the changes that he had initiated:

> Wonderful to be able to appoint keen, bright young teachers includ-
> ing two heads of department and to reflect on the difference it will
> make ... the transfusion is badly needed.

Most curriculum areas were renewed as heads of department were
replaced, less successful teachers left, short-term contracts were
terminated and alternative structures were established. Humanities
(History, Geography, Sociology and RE), Technology (Woodwork,
Metalwork and Textiles) and the Expressive Arts (Art, Drama and
Music) were established, and grouped together a number of previously isolated one or two teacher departments.

Within his overall strategy to 'use HMI inspection as a disciplined
focus to ensure the completion of major changes in systems,
methods and practice', Mr Moore also applied a combination of
pressure and support to individual departments and teachers to
secure improvement. He reckoned that the Hillside staff garden had
never been weeded:

> You are constantly needing to be weeding and planting and the
> garden never looks nice all over. You've always got a patch where
> you're working on it and where you put the new seed in or you've
> transplanted something, or you've got something out of the green-
> house and are putting it in or where, basically, you've got a flame-
> thrower and are clearing the undergrowth.

Senior management monitoring continued to identify inconsistencies in the teaching. In late April, the head and pastoral deputy
between them

> ...observed the first or second half of 22 taught lessons. In their
> judgement, applying Ofsted criteria, 70 per cent of these lessons
> were for the most part satisfactory. Although some teaching was
> excellent, there were common weaknesses affecting a significant
> proportion of the lessons observed.

The 70 per cent figure was lower than that recorded by HMI in
January and the report was critical. 'Few lessons were underway
within ten minutes of the previous bell', while 'too often, teacher ex-
planations are very brief or non-existent' and 'very few of the
observed lessons had an obvious learning outcome. Students were
invited to undertake a variety of activities for no obvious reason,
such as copying pictures from books and answering questions from

textbooks.' The report recommended that: 'Team preparation, team development and team discussion and evaluation are essential if we are to generate the ideas, confidence and energy that will make a difference.' He also acknowledged that 'you can coach people and you can steer people to do things that are constructive but you probably won't make very ineffective teachers into effective ones.'

Powerless and lumbered

Working to finalise the staffing for September, Mr Moore found the LEA unhelpful:

> I'm also concerned that personnel seem to have done nothing about terminating temporary contracts. Nowadays a temporary contract is almost permanent, especially if it runs into a second year, so termination has to be prepared and presented like a redundancy. We are very short of time. So if X or Y decide they've been unfairly treated or realise that their posts are more secure than they seem, I may have quite a problem.

Minor works added to the difficulties. Mr Moore tried to secure LEA approval for a building project. He described the process as 'the Kafkaesque thing'. When Hillside was summoned to an industrial tribunal after a series of mistakes by the personnel division, the head was 'explosive with rage. I feel powerless and lumbered.' He argued that 'if you manage it, you can get it sorted out very quickly but if somebody else manages it, you can't sort it out.' Even basic communications were ineffective: 'Letters, faxes and phone calls seldom elicit prompt responses.'

As LEA inefficiency hindered progress, Mr Moore became increasingly reluctant to be involved in projects that would involve Easton and its officers. When an Education Action Zone was proposed he commented:

> I view the potential for wasted and diverted effort as considerable. Who will be in charge? Who will lead?.

Clive concluded that 'the LEA isn't responding at all. I think they are preoccupied with other issues.' When the LEA came to implement the secondary review proposals, Mr Moore became even more frustrated:

Inspectors were not allowed to play a part in the staffing process for the secondary review, on equal opportunities grounds; they are no longer allowed to assist with capability or competency issues. This means that schools have no access to LEA subject specialist expertise when dealing with poor performance.

Summer monitoring

Shortly before the June HMI monitoring visit, Mr Moore told governors about a major accommodation upgrade and re-organisation, pushed through by Elaine and the retired deputy head who had been working to improve facilities: This included:

- A new staff room, with improved furniture and a free coffee and snacks service

- Eight open plan classrooms being partitioned so that teachers could hear themselves teach

- Two derelict home economics rooms being converted and equipped for use by the humanities faculty

- A drama studio

- A special needs suite

- Departmental and year accommodation, re-grouped so that subject staff and year teams occupied neighbouring classrooms.

Meanwhile the heads of department trained their colleagues in preparation for the monitoring visit. Jenny remembered that they 'had to follow this common approach to writing schemes of work and we had to have a grid to concentrate on ... this was to help staff concentrate on the minutiae of lesson planning'. Mr Moore was confident that these preparations would win HMI approval:

> ...Ofsted like to see the action plan, they like to see the targets, they like to see strategies going for these targets and they like to see in classrooms evidence that everybody is listening and are doing it. So by the time of the last monitoring visit, they see lesson planners on every table, they see homework diaries and planners on every student's desk, they see learning objectives up on walls and it looks like a coherent approach.

The head visited every form, 'urging them to help their teachers do their best on Monday and Tuesday' and told the children that 'I only want three words to go on holiday with, *good progress maintained*'. Despite the extensive preparations, Clive felt the teachers were more relaxed:

> On the evening of the latest monitoring inspection visit it was clear that it was quite a low key affair. I think only eleven lessons were looked at. The head is now in a sense leading the monitoring. What six months ago would have been thought to have been a very threatening process is becoming less so. Now whether that is because people's confidence or even levels of skill are increasing or whether they are learning to play the game remains to be seen.

Only one HMI appeared for the second visit and Mr Moore found himself 'treating him as my father, anxious for approval, adopting expected behaviours. This is near ridiculous in the circumstances and at my age.' He tried to convince the inspector that all the changes, combined with the curriculum, staffing and premises developments, 'will make a different school in the autumn'. The head was doubtful whether the teaching would seem to have improved much since the January visit.

In the event, the HMI asked Mr Moore 'when we'd like the team to come to get us out of special measures'. Jenny thought that although 'staff were exhausted after the HMI visit' they 'were pleased to have been successful and pleased to have an opportunity to get themselves out of special measures'. The oral debrief, followed by a letter from the head of school improvement at Ofsted, confirmed that:

> ...the headteacher, supported by the senior management team, continues to provide strong leadership and clear direction for the work of the school. Staff morale has steadied, is resilient and continues to improve. Behaviour in classrooms is also satisfactory and often good. The headteacher has been resolute in his endeavour to improve teaching. Support to address weaknesses in teaching and proposed staff changes augur well for continual overall improvement.

Good progress had been made with three out of four key issues, with satisfactory progress on the fourth. Mr Moore felt vindicated:

> So when we had a very good report and the fact that now there's the inspection coming in the autumn which will take us out of special measures, I think people are seeing actually the school sitting on so much firmer ground ... all the changes for the teaching are due in the autumn because, basically, there's eleven people gone ... I mean the turn around is sort of thirty per cent of the staff in a year, I think that gave the HMI a feeling the school was going to change very radically.

Although people were tired, they welcomed the social evening arranged for the end of term. Jenny appreciated the fact that only partners were expected to pay: 'Chris has ways of repaying his staff.'

Mr Moore contrasted the July presentation evening with the previous year, when he had attended as a guest:

> Last year's was nice but no refreshments; this year we have drinks before and after; tea, coffee, savoury nibbles. Last year was just prize-winners; this time lots more certificates and the year heads presenting their charges.

Lord of the Rings

The autumn term began with energy and optimism. Elaine commented: 'The impression is that there is new blood in here ... we have got five NQTs alone, two new heads of department ... we have got seven members of staff that have started this year.' She was encouraged to think that:

> We have now got a staff who are fifty per cent not Ofsted scarred. You know they are not the original bunch that went through it so they are not coming with the same baggage, they are not coming with the same history.

Staff turnover was in reality less than Elaine estimated, but it was still significant. Within one year of the original inspection, twenty per cent of the teachers working at Hillside had departed; within two years, thirty five per cent had moved on; within three years, fifty five per cent had left. Within twenty months, six heads of department had left, including the leaders of all the core subjects. Within sixteen months of the inspection, six teachers were affected by long-term illness and none returned to duty. Of the nineteen full and part-time staff serving without responsibility points, fourteen left within three years of the inspection. This contrasted with the eight teachers who left in the two years before the inspection. For Mr Moore, these changes were positive:

> There has been a time lag on the improvement factor in terms of morale. But it was a tremendous start to the year because you had got all these new staff ... most of the heads of department have changed now since the original inspection and the school felt almost normal. A year previously it had felt like there had been a motor crash and people had sat around in chairs ... Walking in here in September it felt like a normal school ... you got laughter when you made jokes.

Elaine was equally optimistic:

> People had worked very hard over the summer to get schemes of work in place ... so that they knew what they were doing, where the departments were going and the new staffing structure was finally setting in with new heads of department taking up their responsibilities. The old senior management team from last year, which Mr Goodlad had put into place the previous year, was now pared down to Mr Moore, Peter and me ... the other three members of the senior management had moved away to be heads of department.

A visiting deputy head from another LEA commented that:

> What I pick up in the staff room is a tremendous buzz of people wanting new ideas and wanting development and wanting things to happen – how on earth was this place in special measures?

Term began with two training days, providing time for departments to work on revised schemes of work and displays for October and November. Teachers were trained to develop their lesson evaluation and feedback skills so they could coach one another towards improved classroom effectiveness.

Like many heads of department, Jenny was not nearly so confident:

> I think the first few weeks of term were very tricky because there was an awful lot to be done and, necessarily, there had to be a tight schedule to get it done in time. What didn't help was that, over and above the normal there was also target setting and we had schemes of work to do for a certain date and then the target setting on top of that and other things to come.

When the LEA inspector came to observe the teaching he reported that 'this is a school very different from the one inspected by Ofsted':

> In every lesson which I observed, pupils were well-behaved and working well, with just a few exceptions. All of the work in classrooms was purposeful and focused. The preferred style of teaching at Hillside tends to be one where the pupils are taught 'at', rather than lessons being part of an ongoing dialogue. There is already evidence that the introduction of drama is playing a significant part in developing a more positive attitude on the part of pupils. The drama lesson I observed was outstanding in several respects.

The public celebration of religious festivals continued, with a major Diwali event before half-term. Year assemblies with student participation followed a careful plan with a thematic approach.

Mr Moore believed that the main improvement stemmed from the new timetable and curriculum. Compared with the previous year, supply teachers had disappeared because there was 'very little illness, very little absence and all the long term sickness disappeared. We had got consistent staff in all the areas.' All the 'peculiarities of the school were disappearing fast. You weren't going to open a door and find five children in a small room.' He was concerned that his colleagues were working too hard and urged them to relax, but it made no difference. As Elaine observed:

> The Friday night before the inspection, Peter and I were throwing people out at 6 o'clock at night because they were still putting up display materials.

Jean reported that 'they were under pressure, under a lot of strain ... but you would still have people working here until 6 o'clock', including Mr Moore who 'did a display board himself ... symbolically important ... senior management making their faces seen around the place ... there was a corporate approach to display.' According to Clive, even the governors found themselves pressurised into a final burst:

> Mr Moore ... pushed the governors very hard to make sure that their visits are made and written up ... governors' agendas have been very carefully constructed to ensure that all ends were covered.

The head was less anxious about the new heads of department:

> Instead of having no leadership in two core subjects for about two years we have suddenly got two very bright and energetic women beavering away all the time and constantly looking for new and better ways of doing things.

In the final stages of preparation, a development plan extension was prepared to cover the next three years. Elaine remembered that three weeks before the inspection Mr Moore gave the staff a 'this is the rules of the game sheet' that he explained and reinforced in the morning briefing. The 'staff script' instructed the teachers in the handling of the inspection:

> Constructive, active engagement with the children should be the prime feature of our work – don't set written tasks which occupy most of the time inspectors are with you. Explain the learning objective ... All student assignments marked up to date.

Although there was a widespread expectation that Hillside would come out of special measures, Mr Moore recorded in his diary that the tension was almost unbearable:

> For many people it was re-visiting the previous Ofsted ... we had teachers vomiting before they came to school, we had teachers who were in a desperately psyched up state. We had teachers who were really frightened.

Jenny later described the experience:

> I think I was the first person observed by one of them ... he was in my next lesson and that was good for me, personally, you know, the worst thing is waiting for them to come – they've seen everybody else. They were as they had been before, silent. I think that's very unnerving. You don't get any feedback whatsoever, blank faced – better than having poor feedback. They were very omnipresent. Even when you were out in the morning, you'd come across somebody walking in the corridors, looking at the displays so that was worth it or you'd be doing duty pre-school, out in the car-park – one of them would be there, you know, they were everywhere, but, in a low-key manner.

The inspection report declared that the school 'no longer requires special measures' and found that in the fifty lessons observed, the teaching in nine out of ten was 'sound or better'; and that in two out of five 'it was good'. After the oral debrief on the third day, Mr Moore called the staff together and told them at once. Elaine remembered that 'people were grinning from ear to ear with a big sense of relief and then we had a bit of a bash for them on the Wednesday night, buns and cake and a glass of wine'. Several people felt that their 'self worth and the school's self worth and everything else had been restored and so they were quite happy', while others, like Jean, were angry they had been put through such a process for the failures of the previous administration:

> Some of the new members of staff, especially the younger ones were really quite joyful. Whereas the older ones and people like me who had been here for the two years almost had a feeling of resentment that they had put us through this process.

Mr Moore 'noticed a wave of Mr Wake stories ... there is a strong sense amongst the staff that they were led into the shit and abandoned there.' Although he was pleased with the result of the inspection, he noticed that 'our teaching became very convergent, much less user-friendly than it needed to be' and reported that the LEA inspector had found the 'amount of exchange between teachers and children in the classrooms was much less than he would have expected. In other words, everybody is following the formula.' He suspected that this was because the staff had experienced 'a very directed management style over the last few months and perhaps forever and we now need to start to carve out the time for more collaborative work'. Heads of department had to become a 'powerful group' because 'it is no good them sitting there waiting to be told what to do'.

After this success, Mr Moore was pressed to stay on, as Mr Goodlad had been. Governors and parents wanted him to build on the success of leaving special measures and to lead the expansion of the school. But he was exhausted:

> Ofsted is the Dark Lord in the educational system and I feel as if I have been a ring bearer ... Frodo can't stay with them because the bearing of the ring is unbearable.

The reckoning
Inspection evidence

The HMI inspection report that released Hillside from special measures (summarised in the Appendix, Table 2, p167) shows a significant improvement in relation to all but one of the key characteristics of effective schools (Sammons *et al.*, 1995), compared with the judgements of the first Ofsted inspection two years earlier (summarised in the Appendix, Table 1, p165). 'Serious shortcomings in the quality of leadership' in the earlier report became 'strong leadership' that gives 'clear direction'. Ofsted had found that leadership failed to 'take a strategic view' but two years later HMI reported that 'the ethos of the school matches its aims'. The first inspection found that 'teachers, by their attitude, provoke bad behaviour', whereas HMI judged that 'the behaviour of pupils in classrooms is good'. A low level of punctuality had 'an adverse effect on attainment and progress'; two years later it was a problem only for a minority, while attendance was better and extra-curricular activities were a strength. Teaching improved from 'a third of lessons are unsatisfactory or poor' to 'the quality ... was sound or better in nine out of ten lessons'. The proportion of lessons found to be 'good' rose from 25 per cent to 40 per cent.

Ofsted had found that expectations were 'low and the pace of teaching is slow'. Two years on, HMI reported that the head was judged to have been 'resolute in his endeavour to improve teaching. Support in order to address weaknesses in teaching, and staff changes, have proved beneficial for continual overall improvement'. Weak provision for 'spiritual, moral, social and cultural development' was replaced by 'moral and social development' that was 'good'. Ofsted inspectors reported that 'the school does not evaluate its work systematically' but two years later 'the work of the school is monitored and evaluated in a systematic way'. Pupils used to have 'few opportunities ... to take responsibility for themselves or for others' but by the time of the HMI report they were found to 'demonstrate a worthy sense of values and show respect for each other's views'. The school had 'taken a number of initiatives to reflect and celebrate the multicultural nature of the school population'.

Ofsted believed that Hillside was not a learning organisation because 'the amount of staff development and contact with a range of sources of new ideas and expertise is low' but this, too, had changed. HMI judged that 'Staff have worked hard to improve the school. They feel valued and confident, and morale is high. The school has the capacity for self-improvement'.

Seven months after Hillside came out of special measures, two HMI visited as part of the Easton LEA inspection and observed eight lessons. They also conducted interviews with senior staff. Their remarks further confirm the improved character of the school:

> Seven of the eight lessons observed were good or very good; the eighth was satisfactory but showed insecure subject knowledge ... the teaching was impressive overall. Lessons were well prepared and planned; there was a clear focus on objectives; targets were set. Questioning and direct teaching/explanation were good ... Expectations were high and right ... Although all the classes seen were of lower ability they listened well, especially in drama, and picked up on the teachers' expectations. Attainment was low because of the nature of the groups but progress was satisfactory or good ... HMI further commented on the school's progress since the November inspection which brought Hillside out of special measures. They believe the school is continuing to improve. Work with subject leaders has been effective.

Student outcomes

Hillside attempted to demonstrate the impact on student outcomes of these improved organisational characteristics. The attendance figures had reached a low point in Mr Wake's last full year (85.7 per cent) but had recovered to 88.4 per cent by the time he left, despite the considerable turbulence arising from the Ofsted inspection and the closure threat. This placed the school 2.5 per cent below the national average attendance for England of 90.9 per cent. Although considerable resources were directed into monitoring and managing attendance during the two years in special measures, as the action plan required, attendance only improved another one per cent in the first year and point nine per cent in the second.

The year before the Ofsted inspection there were five fixed term exclusions and seven permanent exclusions. This compares with sixty-eight fixed term and six permanent exclusions in Mr Moore's first year.

Records of student performance are incomplete, mainly because the process of bench-marking, recording and evaluating progress did not become fully operational until the spring of Mr Moore's first year. Table 1 (p130) presents the details available for the cohorts that graduated from Hillside from the year before the study to the year after the study. The information is drawn from the Access database constructed by Mr Moore.

Hillside's performance at GCSE, measured by the percentage of students achieving five or more higher grades, fluctuated in relation to national and local averages as shown in Table 2 (p131).

The proportion of students obtaining no GCSE qualification was thirteen per cent in three of the five years shown in Table 1, significantly below national or local averages at the time. The proportion obtaining five GCSE grades A* to G was the same in the summer before the Ofsted inspection as it was when Mr Moore left.

The mean key stage 2 levels in English, mathematics and science achieved by students entering Hillside were similar each year. The mean key stage 3 level attained in English rose by 1.3 over three years but the levels for mathematics and science varied little. Mean CAT and Reading Age scores were consistent through the three years of the study, indicating a student cohort with an ability profile well below the national average, as might be expected from the free meals entitlement shown in Table 1 (overleaf).

These disappointing figures did not alter the inspectors' overall opinion that special measures were no longer required. The test and examination results are puzzling nevertheless. Official models judge school effectiveness by results and measure improvement by gains in value-added performance. At Hillside, improvements in observed effectiveness seem to have produced no significant change in student outcomes. Chapter seven analyses the evidence about the school's apparent transformation described in these pages and explores the reality behind the figures. What lessons can be learned from this case study?

Table 1: Hillside School Student Data (Year 11)

	Year before study	1st year of study	2nd year of study	3rd year of study	Year after study@
Free School Meal Uptake	n/a	18%	15%	16%	17%
GCSE 5A*-C	27%	41%	34%	31%	21%
GCSE 5A*-G	78%	82%	80%	78%	77%
GCSE No Passes	13%	13%	8%	13%	11%
Key Stage 3 English mean level	n/a	n/a	3.4	3.8	4.6
Key Stage 3 Maths mean level	n/a	n/a	4.2	4.2	4.2
Key Stage 3 Science mean level	n/a	n/a	4.3	4.1	4.4

@The results in this column relate to Hillside after its expansion.

n/a: Not available.

Table 2: Hillside School Students: Percentage Achieving 5 GCSE A*-C Grades Compared with National and Local Averages

	Year before study	1st year of study	2nd year of study	3rd year of study
Hillside cf national average	-17.5	-4.1	-12.3	-16.9
Hillside cf local average	n/a	+8.2	-0.8	-6.1

7

Learning from Hillside

What happened?

Hillside's improvement journey ends with a sense of both triumph and disappointment. HMI monitoring and the final inspection report describe remarkable improvements in terms of the effectiveness criteria routinely used to measure quality. With special measures left behind, Hillside was set to expand, not close. A new, vibrant culture seems to have been established and was beginning to bear fruit in the classroom. Lessons were found impressive overall and the capacity for further improvement was recognised. Compared with two years before, the school was transformed.

A nagging doubt remains, however, despite the optimism of the inspectors and everyone involved. The best GCSE headline performance was achieved when Hillside was in chaos, while the main quantitative indicators failed to show a progressive trend at any stage during the school's recovery. There is at least a suspicion that the transformation may have been an illusion, produced in the artificial environment of special measures and resting on a flattering contrast with the long term decline experienced under Mr Wake. The apparently dramatic changes described in the study may not have been deep enough to bring about a measurable increase in classroom effectiveness. Important questions arise, however. What lessons can be learned about how heads bring about such impressive changes in the observed effectiveness of their schools? How should the absence of quantifiable improvement influence our interpretation of transformations like those at Hillside? Each section of the analysis below concludes with recommendations for action by schools, leaders and government agencies.

Why did Hillside fail?

Eye witnesses are clear about the reasons for Hillside's decline and failure. Mr Wake's authoritarian philosophy, intimidating manner and his pessimism and personal disillusionment permeated the school and the lives of the teachers and children. His unpredictable moods and inconsistent decisions, particularly over pupil discipline, created a climate in which people were wary and reluctant to engage in open debate. He saw meetings with other heads as a waste of time and discouraged his colleagues from participating in all forms of professional development. He resented the influence of local authority officers and advisers, while the governing body was structured so that it could exert no significant influence on the conduct of the school. Although the local authority, some parents and many teachers were well aware of the problematic nature of the head's leadership, no one successfully challenged him before the intervention of Ofsted.

Within a rigid, unchanging structure, Mr Wake delegated administration to his deputy and the curriculum to heads of department. He made no attempt, however, to ensure a fair distribution of roles and responsibilities or to coordinate policy and practice. Although a loose management structure appeared to empower middle managers, confidence was undermined by unpredictable, irascible interventions. Hillside did not respond to changes in the local environment, so that the shifting composition of the intake and the increasing cultural diversity in the school were ignored. Long-serving teachers and senior managers aged together, given few opportunities to refresh their understanding of management or teaching and learning. As the school's reputation declined, it became unattractive for new pupils and staff so that, increasingly, vulnerable teachers were recruited.

Mr Wake's uncomfortable regime confirms the idea that climate and motivation are closely related to leadership styles (Litwin and

Stringer, 1968). His bossy, coercive method aroused the negativity of his colleagues and inhibited what could be achieved. At Hillside, a distinctive culture was built over twenty years as followers adapted to Mr Wake's behaviour and decisions. A head's stories and choices about who should be promoted, what should be measured and who should be excluded are 'primary embedding mechanisms' (Schein, 2004) that influence people's long-term expectations of themselves and others.

Lack of trust was an intrinsic part of this culture, particularly after the teachers' industrial dispute of the mid-eighties. Following union instructions, most of the staff had withdrawn from lunch duties and extra-curricular activities in pursuit of a pay claim. Mr Wake interpreted their behaviour as unforgivable disloyalty and for the rest of his time at the school ran lunch time as if the union action had continued indefinitely. Like Mr Wake and his colleagues, leaders and followers can be frozen into patterns of behaviour that are unrelated to their environment and are consequently disposed to dismiss evidence that does not fit with their assumptions about the world.

Ofsted inspection destroyed Mr Wake's remaining credibility as governors, teachers and the wider community absorbed the shocking reality of special measures. Failure produced an overriding imperative for change missing from many coasting, cruising or otherwise complacent schools, where similar but less marked characteristics may be found. Ofsted is a powerful instrument for dealing with entrenched attitudes and cultures that have become grimly unproductive for those who work within them. Although the psychological cost for many teachers is high, special measures can clear the ground for improvement or even transformation.

How do successful heads lead?
The striking contrast between the Jekyll and Hyde-like conduct of Mr Wake and the relentlessly optimistic style adopted by Mr Goodlad and Mr Moore shows that active engagement and personal warmth are essential characteristics for successful school leaders. The new heads adopted a self-consciously different approach from Mr Wake and presented themselves as energetic, encouraging and keen to value their colleagues. Teachers, students and parents were

motivated by confident, upbeat styles and were frustrated by controlling behaviour and pessimistic attitudes. All this confirms the model of leadership recommended by the NCSL (2003). Highly effective heads adopt combinations of personal characteristics and leadership styles that match the situations they encounter. Mr Goodlad and Mr Moore deliberately switched interpersonal strategies and styles to deal with particular individuals and circumstances. They were not afraid to coach the strong and dislodge the weak, while maintaining a generally encouraging atmosphere.

As a result, the climate at the school steadily improved. The two incoming heads emphasised actions that relate closely to the six climate dimensions identified by Hay Group (NCSL, 2003):

- *Flexibility.* New ideas were generated through the staff working groups

- *Responsibility.* Teachers were given enhanced roles and responsibilities through the action plan

- *Standards* of achievement were stressed by senior managers through the audit process

- *Rewards.* Praise was more frequent than blame and was related to individual contributions (e.g. organising an event)

- *Clarity.* Expectations were clarified and communicated through regular meetings and formal documentation

- *Team Commitment.* Festivals, celebrations and volunteer groups encouraged teachers, students and parents to work together in effective teams.

This improving climate did not motivate everyone, however. The teachers at Hillside were not all alike, clean slates poised for the arrival of a positive leader equipped with an approved repertoire of styles. On the contrary, there were winners, like Elaine and Peter, who attached themselves to the new heads and found exciting opportunities for influence and action, and there were losers, like Sidney and Gerald, who lacked the energy and will to reinvent themselves. Over one third of the staff left within eighteen months of the inspection. These people would have found the lightest touch coercive and oppressive, mainly because they rejected the agenda imposed on the school by external pressures.

The heads themselves did not always adopt a neat, well-judged selection of styles designed to arouse the achievement motive, as recommended by the NCSL. In their respective ways, both sometimes resembled the 'shapers' who broke all the human relations rules. They were:

> ...abounding in nervous energy and actuated by the need for achievement ... they were the antithesis of team men. They challenged; argued; disagreed. They were impatient and easily frustrated. Their proneness to aggression would produce a reciprocal reaction from other team members... (Belbin, 1981, p59)

Mr Goodlad challenged the staff through the students and drove impulsively through conventional procedures, leaving some people bemused and dissatisfied. Less capable teachers found Mr Moore's direct involvement in the monitoring process oppressive, especially when he followed a classroom visit by confronting them with evidence of poor performance. Mr Moore was manipulative in dealing with the governors when they wanted to reinstate an excluded pupil and manoeuvred to by-pass members of the senior management team when he considered them untrustworthy or unhelpful.

There is also a danger that the current emphasis on human relations skills, particularly in programmes like LPSH, has created a limited perspective on headship and has led to the neglect of the bureaucratic, professional and moral sources of authority available to heads as they seek to influence their schools (Sergiovanni, 1995).

The new heads mobilised all these strands to achieve their vision and goals. Mr Goodlad used his position to steer through major changes, apologising in advance but not troubling to consult many of those affected. His professional experience enabled him to construct a convincing action plan and he appealed to child-centred values when removing the chains from the doors at lunch-time. Mr Moore's vision was based on equal value and equal opportunity and he used his professional expertise to engineer new staff and curriculum structures that realised his aims. Hodgkinson (1991, p112) argues that:

> ...the deadliest weapons in the administrative armoury are philosophical: the skills of logical and critical analysis, conceptual synthesis, value analysis and commitment, the power of expression in

language and communication, rhetoric and, most fundamentally, the depth of understanding of human nature.

Without such weapons, Mr Moore could not have negotiated an accommodation between his faith in comprehensive education and the demands of the government machine. He would not have known how to reconcile targets and festivals and would have been unable to win moral support for the struggle with Ofsted and the LEA. Like Mr Wake, he would have avoided dealing with the value dilemmas he faced (e.g. dealing with poor performance) by ignoring them.

Although the NCSL recognises 'personal conviction' as a source of motivation for headteachers, the main leadership programmes are not concerned with the particular values and professional philosophy that may shape the priorities and decisions of an individual headteacher, nor with the moral complexity of the situations that may be encountered. A leader's 'social democratic or liberal humanist' values (Earley and Weindling, 2004, p61) should not be seen as convictions to be imposed regardless of the context but as an ethical perspective to guide the process of negotiation through which dilemmas are resolved (Day *et al.*, 2000). Mr Moore persuaded his subject heads that flexible grouping had advantages over banding but chose not to press mixed ability, his own preferred solution. He understood the strength and importance of the Asian community however, and yielded nothing to those who objected to celebrating Diwali. Consideration of these issues has yielded the following recommendations.

Recommendations

■ Heads should adopt a variety of styles adapted to the people and situations they encounter. They should recognise that their own habits (impatience, need to please) have a larger-than-life impact on others.

■ Senior managers should work to strengthen the climate of the school, with particular emphasis on clarity and standards.

■ Positive relationships are important but are not the exclusive key to success. School leaders should deepen their understanding of the values that may lead to conflicts and dilemmas in educational settings.

- Office confers positional power over people, information and resources. Heads should distribute as much power as possible to other managers.

- School leaders at all levels should seek honest feedback on their performance. Do not wait for formal appraisal.

- Avoid inconsistency and unfairness. Students and teachers complain most when they feel the boss does not treat them justly.

- People should to be asked rather than told.

How do leaders develop trust?

Without mutual respect for one another's competence and trustworthiness, leaders and followers are unlikely to share and coordinate power effectively (Fullan, 2003). Hillside illustrates the extent to which a school can be crippled by lack of trust. After Ofsted, the staff felt that Mr Wake had led them up a creek and abandoned them there without a paddle. He even lacked the courage to tell them the result, which did not emerge until the registered inspector presented his report to the governing body. Many teachers felt equally let down by the LEA, which they felt should have intervened earlier to deal with problems that were well known to county advisers. As a result of these feelings the staff finally participated in Mr Wake's departure – by writing to the chair of governors to express their lack of confidence in his ability to lead the school out of special measures.

Mr Goodlad's abrupt arrival did not improve matters immediately. As he had been drafted in by an apparently untrustworthy LEA, some teachers believed he was part of a conspiracy to close the school. Others, worried about criticism of their departments in the inspection report, were reluctant to trust a head who was determined to implement an Ofsted agenda. The new head's charisma won over parents and children more quickly than the staff, some of whom remained suspicious. But his vigorous actions soon convinced people that he was determined to save the school. Teachers who were given responsibilities quickly adjusted to the new regime; others remained wary. As Mr Goodlad raced to improve the school and generate a case for keeping it open, those who seemed world-weary or lacking in confidence were displaced or left behind.

Mr Moore recognised at once that he could achieve nothing without the trust of the apprehensive colleagues who had been shaken by the events of the summer. Mutual confidence was the key to everything else. Swiftly assessing the character of the two temporary deputies, he concluded that they had the skill to bring about the improvements that were so badly needed. Mr Moore was also impressed by their judgement and noticed how much the staff trusted them. He made their deputy headships permanent and drew them into a close partnership. The three met each morning to discuss all that was going on and coordinated plans to deal with problems and difficulties as they arose.

Chris Moore set up groups and held meetings to share information and build confidence in open decision making. He personally disclosed information, even when the news was very bad (e.g. disastrous budget, possible redundancies), and explained how his mind was working on possible escape routes. He aimed to earn trust by listening to the concerns of his staff and by demonstrating his commitment to their welfare and future, however bleak things might seem. Like Churchill offering 'blood, sweat and tears', he understood the value of grim truth when you are fighting for survival.

The impact was not uniformly positive. He could not disown the Ofsted action plan, though he condemned the government's policy of 'naming and shaming' failing schools. He was eager to be seen to support struggling teachers and emphasised a positive, blame free culture but he also applied pressure to the less capable and discontinued the temporary contracts of those he perceived to lack capability. The senior management team had an inner and outer group because he did not have faith in all of the members who had been appointed under Mr Goodlad. He never achieved the degree of mutual trust with Julian, Graham and Donna, for example, that existed between the members of the kitchen cabinet. Trust between leaders and followers is a two-way relationship and without it there can be no constructive teamwork and action.

Recommendations

■ Heads should behave in such a way that their values and priorities are clear and consistent. Leaders and followers build trust and mutual respect through successful action in assigned roles. Distributed leadership is impossible without trust.

■ Heads should share information and the thinking behind their plans and decisions. Team members need to understand the leader's theory of action. Why is it right to do this?

■ Schools should ensure that their values are agreed and made explicit so that they guide decisions about priorities.

■ Dilemmas (e.g. exclusion, curriculum options) are a test of agreed values and should be discussed openly unless they compromise particular individuals.

How was leadership distributed?

Mr Wake's delegation to his deputy and the heads of department shows that although distributed leadership has been around for a long time, there is no guarantee that devolved responsibility leads to effective management or to improved outcomes for students (Harris, 2004). Although Mr Wake gave some individuals an extensive range of duties, their sphere of action was undefined. Tasks were handed down but no teams were formally organised or co-ordinated. One teacher did not realise that he had become head of department until a pay rise appeared on his salary slip. Meetings were controlled by the head and the atmosphere was not conducive to proper discussion of policy. The organisation was therefore informal and loosely-coupled (Weick, 1988). Low levels of vertical integration and horizontal coordination ensured that no initiative could be effectively implemented beyond the remit of a single department, although individuals seemed to have ample scope for action.

Mr Goodlad was eager to involve teachers in the campaign to implement the action plan and save the school. He rewarded those who accepted responsibility for a goal or target with promotion points and set up the pupil progress and curriculum teams to develop improved policies and practice. He created a senior management team to coordinate all the work required to match Ofsted requirements.

During his first autumn Mr Moore was keen to make these teams work. He established an overarching structure with senior managers leading groups of governors and teachers, and provided further opportunities for involvement through the volunteer groups on ethos, tutoring and mentoring, curriculum and communications. The head and deputies also worked with individuals and departments to stimulate change and they intervened frequently to challenge unsatisfactory practice and to remove obstacles to progress.

Although tempted to be more directly involved in policy-making, Mr Moore resisted the desire to interfere with working group proposals. The curriculum scheme, for example, was less consistent with his concept of entitlement than he wished but he realised that late changes would undermine what Elaine had achieved through her leadership of the group. He acknowledged that the validity of the exercise depended on enabling groups to see their recommendations fully implemented. Peter was supported in the same way, as the tutoring group developed new ideas for the pastoral system.

Mr Wake had avoided structures that might constrain his right to decide, while Mr Moore deliberately designed stable, predictable frameworks and criteria (e.g. staff structure, exclusion procedures) that would guide decision-making and avoid the need for frequent personal interventions by the head. He shaped leadership roles so that the deputies and senior teachers understood their strategic responsibility for planning and coordination. The senior management audit institutionalised a close monitoring regime that checked the implementation and progress of policy initiatives and supplied information for review and development. These arrangements provided a suitable foundation for effective distributed leadership.

Recommendations

■ Leaders should ensure that policies and practices are consistent with the school's agreed values.

■ Leaders should coordinate and align the structures, systems, people and resources necessary to achieve planned objectives.

■ Leaders should also coordinate the implementation of new policies and monitor progress towards goals.

■ Basic systems (e.g. staff and student discipline, appointments and promotions) should be documented so that there are consistent rules about procedure.

■ Heads should establish audit systems to ensure that policies are implemented effectively.

How was the school's capacity improved?

The immediate impact of Ofsted was to reduce the capacity of the school. Dysfunctional arrangements ceased to work at all as early retirement and long-term sickness swept away experience, knowledge and memory. The closure decision produced anxiety, instability and planning blight, so that many of the teachers who remained were to some extent emotionally incapacitated. Even the best teachers felt that there was a permanent stain on their professional record. As there is a constant shortage of teachers who are prepared to work in challenging circumstances, the wastage of experienced professionals at Hillside (fifty-five per cent in three years) raises questions about the overall benefits of 'naming', 'shaming' and reorganising struggling schools. Improved capacity at a particular site has to be balanced against a substantial net loss of teachers to the system.

At Hillside, nevertheless, the closure decision and the manoeuvres that followed had an energising effect. The local community was drawn into the school and governors began to recognise that they had been insufficiently active. Individual members of staff saw an opportunity to play a part in the school's future, either by joining the parent campaign or by adding to the pressure on Mr Wake to leave. Those who seized this opportunity ceased to be victims. The combination of special measures and closure also licensed the new heads to play heroic commanding roles with governors, parents and colleagues, who were searching for someone with the professional expertise to guide them out of the wilderness. Threats to the school's survival stimulated the sense of urgency needed for successful change and helped create the conditions for later capacity-building and improvement (Kotter, 1996).

Mr Goodlad encouraged and harnessed this new-found energy by bringing people together in assemblies, briefings, open days and committee meetings. He supported initiatives with time, space and resources and glowed with approval when an event was a success. People knew what was happening and for the first time were able to contribute. The action plan provided a structure for improving the school, with new teams established and goals set. External consultants, peer observation and training courses related to the action plan aimed to enhance the knowledge, awareness and skills of the staff.

With more time at his disposal, Mr Moore developed these new practices into standard features of the school. Governor committees enabled members to monitor Hillside's progress on the budget, the action plan and the development of the curriculum. Staff working groups drew on the energy and commitment freed up by the events of the summer, producing numerous policies and ideas. A common approach to teaching and learning was agreed and implemented; the new deputy heads were trained in the skills they needed for their unfamiliar roles; and staff felt valued because they were involved in decision-making. Mr Moore provided training to support innovation in information technology and the expressive arts as well as to improve basic classroom skills.

Both Mr Goodlad and Mr Moore had no doubt that with thirty per cent of lessons at the school found to be unsatisfactory, weak teachers had to be improved or removed. As deputy responsible for the curriculum, Elaine was doubtful whether these inadequate teachers had the ability to change. She suggested that the worst teachers seemed to be 'bonkers' and were too preoccupied with their own problems to manage children effectively. There were limits to what could be achieved by guidance and support. But Mr

Moore applied relentless pressure, demanding that lessons comply with the 'common approach' by following a basic structure that included a beginning, middle and end. Sometimes he was rewarded by an addition to the long-term sick list or another hard to fill vacancy. He remained determined, nevertheless, to get 'the right people on the bus, the wrong people off the bus, and the right people in the right seats' (Collins, 2001, p12) because he understood so well that one negative team member could derail all that he was trying to achieve (Kotter, 1996).

Mr Moore was uncomfortable in combining the roles of inspiring leader, mentor and source of pressure. He empathised with struggling teachers and felt that he should use his coaching skills to help them. When mentoring failed, however, the head found himself in an impossible dilemma. Should he continue the emotional support the teacher expected, or invoke the capability procedures? Mr Moore's usual decisiveness could be blunted by his humane concern that some of the least effective teachers also suffered from depression and stress-related illness. David Brown, for example, survived despite obvious weaknesses in his teaching.

Once the school's future was secure and permanent appointments could be made, Hillside began to improve rapidly. Administrative staff like the office and business managers hastened to replace moribund systems. Well-qualified, energetic teachers, untouched by past traumas, began to tackle neglected issues in organising and delivering the curriculum. The head and deputies now supported a team of trusted middle managers and ensured that technical expertise and resources were available for new schemes and initiatives. Small departments were grouped together to reduce the isolation of individual teachers and to improve curriculum coherence. A combination of enhanced motivation, structural reorganisation, intensive professional development and the introduction of new skills from outside produced an impressive capacity for continuing improvement.

Recommendations

- Post-holders responsible for particular tasks and processes should be identified, and their line management and group leadership responsibilities should be set out in writing.

- Senior managers should lead volunteer working groups in policy review and development. Their proposals should be implemented in full.

- Arrangements for performance management, peer observation and review, coaching, mentoring and training should be clarified so that those concerned are clear about what is expected of them; and so that individual members of staff are aware of their entitlement (e.g. for NQT support).

- Heads should ensure that the school has an integrated approach to recruitment, retention, development and succession planning. They should be aware of individual and group life-cycles and should consider how to refresh teams that are no longer performing well.

- Training should be related to the needs of the school and the individual so that appropriate skills (e.g. financial and curriculum analysis, data management) are available when required.

- Heads should tackle obstacles to improvement – a vacancy is better than resistant attitudes and poor teaching.

How do leaders improve quality in the classroom?

The improvement in the quality of teaching at Hillside was marked. During the first Ofsted inspection, a third of the lessons were unsatisfactory and teachers were seen to provoke bad behaviour. Only two years later, the teaching was considered 'impressive overall' and the proportion of good lessons had almost doubled. How was this achieved?

Mr Wake's portrait of himself as a teaching head and track-suited manager is at first sight puzzling. He delegated administrative responsibility so that he could devote himself to a substantial time-tabled commitment and he was directly involved with the children through his role at lunchtime. Departments were given considerable freedom, provided they generated no visible cause for concern. He contrasted his approach with that of other heads who were bogged down in administration and had no time for their students. Why did this method not produce more effective results in the classroom?

The answer seems to be that Mr Wake's method was too personal and that he failed to follow through his declared concern for teaching and learning by visiting classrooms or by taking an interest in professional practice and development. Mr Wake's own teaching seems to have isolated him from the work of the school, while his frequently repetitive or cancelled assemblies set a poor example for teachers and children. Subject departments were not coordinated or monitored; there was no overarching view of teaching and learning. The result, revealed by the Ofsted inspection, was inconsistency, with many pockets of poor practice.

Mr Moore's intense, detailed efforts to improve teaching and learning could not have been more different. He had no timetabled classes and was seldom scheduled for cover. Instead, he worked ceaselessly with groups and individuals to improve all the dimensions that contribute to effective classroom learning. He coached heads of department in the skills of writing schemes of work and classroom observation. He steered Elaine towards an entitlement curriculum and ensured that inefficient small classes no longer continued. On the basis of regular monitoring and observation, he intervened at departmental and classroom level to ensure a 'common approach' to lessons and teaching that was coordinated, consistent and effective. He acted directly to remove ineffectual team leaders and teachers.

Mr Moore's strong emphasis on his 'leading professional' role, and his success in improving the quality of teaching and learning, show that determined heads need not succumb to organisational pressures or the burdens of administration reported in the literature (Wolcott, 1984). His approach also provides some evidence that the boundary between 'professional' and 'executive' roles may be less clear than Hughes (1998) and Doughty (1998) suggest. A distinctive educational strategy was served, for example, by his decision to reduce expenditure on keeping classes small and to increase departmental spending on books and equipment. Mr Moore's 'executive' effort to secure partitions for eight open plan classrooms was a visible demonstration of his commitment and values, and enhanced the quality of teaching, whereas his more obviously 'professional' attempts to improve David Brown's lessons failed to do so.

This case study therefore confirms the belief that:

> The principal's interest in instructional matters and program and organisational planning is critical ... the schools in which principals showed a direct interest in instruction were significantly more likely to show gains in student achievement. (Fullan, 1982, p137)

The improved quality of teaching and learning at Hillside seems to be directly related to Mr Moore's remorseless emphasis on lessons and to his endeavours to organise and direct resources to achieve the best possible combination of teachers, training, facilities and equipment at classroom level. He coordinated people, policies and practices so that the curriculum, schemes of work and individual lessons were aligned with one another and were consistent with the objectives that had been agreed in the beginning. Special measures seem to concentrate the mind on the quality and consistency of classroom teaching, with frequently startling results. Hillside, like other schools that have been turned round (see Hampton and Jones, 2000), shows that dramatic changes can be achieved. Whether such changes can be sustained when the original crisis has faded from memory is another matter.

Recommendations

■ Heads should ensure a continuous, remorseless focus on the classroom, even when there is no apparent cause for concern or complaint.

■ Heads should integrate their professional and administrative responsibilities so that the school's values, budget, curriculum, staffing structure, facilities and resources are aligned to achieve the best possible combination for effective learning.

- Up-to-date professional learning and development should enhance classroom practice.

- Monitoring, evaluation and feedback should inform plans for further improvement.

Do students make a difference?

Although one visitor thought that the students were 'pussy cats' compared with the children at many city schools, the heads and teachers at Hillside believed that their work was seriously constrained by student variables. Mr Wake and his senior colleagues claimed that the academic quality of the intake was in decline. Mr Moore felt that he was a social worker trying to 'keep the lid' on problems that were wide and deep. Students were increasingly drawn from disadvantaged wards where there was a high incidence of poor housing, poor health, unemployment and premature death. Over twenty per cent of students qualified for free meals. A similar proportion came from homes where English was not the first language. After the closure announcement, the school had to accept a significant number of 'recycled' children whose record often included violence and truancy.

Mr Wake's response to these growing problems was to engineer small bottom sets where slow learners received extra help and poor behaviour could be contained. Able students were placed in top sets where lessons were not disrupted by those with limited ability and poor concentration. He was personally sympathetic to problem students and their families but exasperated year heads by his willingness to give second and third chances to challenging individuals who had ruined lessons. Mr Wake did not expect troublesome students to obtain GCSE grades and saw the problem in terms of containment.

Although Mr Moore was saddened by the personal circumstances of some disruptive individuals and their families, he was rigorous in applying the behaviour code and worked hard to build a systematic, consistent approach to every aspect of tutoring, mentoring and disciplining students. Hillside began to expect everyone to achieve. Lunch clubs, sports and outdoor adventure activities were introduced to counter disaffection. An entitlement curriculum with flexible grouping replaced the bottom sets, while alternative vocational courses were provided for those who struggled with written subjects.

Despite these initiatives, misbehaviour in the classroom and fights in corridors and the playground continued to create disturbances, especially when the teachers concerned were less than capable. Lateness and truancy absorbed professional time and energy in different ways. Costly systems were established to monitor and encourage regular attendance but the number of missing students remained stubbornly high, especially amongst low achievers in years ten and eleven, who believed they had no hope of GCSE success.

When the governors reinstated a student who was alleged to have stabbed a teacher, Mr Moore worked to contain the explosive potential of the incident, negotiating with the assailant, parents, governors and staff to avoid a breakdown in relationships and to find a solution acceptable to all parties. The near-disaster threatened by this episode, and the great importance attached to its resolution by everyone involved, illuminates the significance of pastoral case work in schools in 'challenging circumstances'. Angry students who carry the burden of their past experience into the classroom and playground can threaten a school's stability. Senior managers know instinctively that their priority is to preserve delicate relationships that have been pushed towards the edge, even at the cost of neglecting lessons and plans to improve the school. Their success adds nothing to the improvement measured by performance tables and targets but their failure may precipitate even more serious disturbance.

Hillside supports the conclusion of recent research (Lupton, 2004) that an unbalanced, relatively disadvantaged intake can have a cumulatively negative impact on student outcomes. The school illustrates how external social and cultural influences permeate school boundaries, mould internal processes and distract students and teachers from educational objectives. Social geography seems to limit what leaders can achieve and to exert a greater influence than an individual school's curriculum and internal organisation. (Levačić and Woods, 2002a, 2002b).

Recommendations

■ Government agencies should be realistic about the influence of intake mix on the character and success of schools in disadvantaged areas. When the balance is positive, all students perform above expectations; when the balance is negative, the quality of learning is compromised for everyone.

■ Despite all discouragement, school leaders should maintain a positive approach to tutoring, mentoring and student discipline. If you neglect problems they get worse. Government agencies should be much more willing to recognise and praise teachers who support students in challenging circumstances.

■ School leaders should work to enhance the curriculum so that there are relevant opportunities for all. Activities, adventures, trips and visits can enhance motivation, reduce disaffection and encourage students' commitment to learning.

Does intervention help or hinder change?

Hillside illustrates how the national agenda conditions the behaviour of heads at supposedly self-managing schools. Determined to deal with failure and raise performance, government agencies and the local authority engineered imperatives and expectations that informed almost every decision at the school. Even the governors' choice of a leader to follow Mr Wake was prejudiced by the LEA's refusal to agree a permanent appointment and by Ofsted's (2001) emphasis on 'strong' leaders who 'turn round' troubled schools.

The Ofsted framework provided a compelling definition of the changes that were required and encouraged a rigorous approach to poor teaching that might have been more difficult in a less precarious, less supervised environment. HMI monitoring visits became staging posts in the school's progress towards recovery, and enabled Mr Moore and his team to adjust priorities appropriately as action plan targets were achieved. The head, deputies and the heads of department knew exactly what was expected of them and were stimulated to adopt an unusually tightly-coupled organisation that might have been less acceptable in a school with a stronger track record of success.

External pressures were also destructive. As staff later complained, the trauma and disruption of inspection and threatened closure were heavy-handed responses to a leadership problem that the LEA should have resolved long before. Many teachers perceived themselves as scapegoats for the former head and the systems that failed to hold him accountable, and saw special measures as a punishment rather than as support for improvement. As we have seen, some were permanently marked by their sense of shame and injustice; others became ill and left the profession; almost everyone felt that an alien language and irrelevant priorities had been imposed on them. Teachers began to accept and work towards objectives defined by Ofsted, but they were never reconciled to the bureaucratic rationality implicit in the special measures regime.

Easton LEA's determination to remove surplus places and improve the quality of local provision also contributed to the dynamic of change. The closure decision, made without any formal procedure or consultation, set up the dialectic between the internal and external processes that followed. As the boundary imploded, the multiple, competing agendas of Easton LEA, Ofsted and the DfEE threatened to overwhelm what remained of the school's capacity for self-management, and stimulated teachers and the local community to protest against the organs and agencies of government.

Hillside's transformation was produced in the context of a prolonged struggle for survival, in which school-based participants saw the conventional agents of improvement (LEA, Ofsted) as malign forces to be fought with their own weapons (e.g. action plan, targets). The LEA's undeveloped systems and procedures provided the heads at Hillside with room for manoeuvre as they aimed to counter threats and exploit opportunities. But ineffective and inefficient services also made change more difficult to achieve, especially in relation to personnel and building issues, as a subsequent inspection of Easton LEA confirmed.

Recommendations

- ■ Government agencies should recognise that their own agendas and activities – regulation, funding streams, inspection, tests and performance tables – reduce the choices available to school leaders and set up a perpetual tension between internal and external priorities.

- ■ Policy-makers should acknowledge the emotional cost of intervention to improve schools, such as serious weaknesses, special measures. How can capable teachers be protected against fall-out? Should intervention be targeted with greater precision? Should an early warning system be established to identify at-risk leadership and management?

- ■ Policy-makers should recognise that current funding levels have compromised the ability of LEAs to maintain effective services and support schools in challenging circumstances.

- ■ Local authorities should be aware of the planning blight and demoralisation associated with proposals for school reorganisation. Many capable teachers – usually in mid to late career – can be lost to the system, while the education of children across a whole city can be compromised for several years. What are the quantifiable benefits? Are they guaranteed?

Why didn't the examination results improve?

Neither Mr Goodlad nor Mr Moore were able to convert their 'strong leadership' and the school's new-found 'capacity for self-improvement' (HMI Inspection Report) into better academic results. Despite a comprehensive reform programme designed to enhance characteristics linked to student achievement (Sammons *et al.*, 1995), there was no significant change to the figures shown in Table 1 (p130).

Although there were annual variations in test and examination results, there is no sign of an upward trend on any measure, except the Key Stage 3 English mean. The best GCSE 5 A* – C outcome was achieved during the first year of the study by the cohort most likely to have been affected by poor teaching and disruption. Hillside was seventeen per cent behind the national average GCSE performance in the year before the study and sixteen point nine per cent behind when the study ended (see Table 2, p131). No other quantifiable measure improved either, such as attendance and exclusions.

To conclude that Hillside's measurable effectiveness was un-changed may not be the whole story, however. Many teachers be-lieved that a good many of the most able students left the school during the closure crisis. Though the headline GCSE figures did not change, the fact that they did not fall may suggest an improved value-added performance by year groups which became progres-sively more disadvantaged each year. Unfortunately this cannot be tested because the available data is incomplete, especially for the students who graduated before the Access database was fully operational. Another possible explanation is that the study may have concluded before the main improvements had time to affect classroom performance.

Alternatively, HMI may have been wrong. Although observers, participants and inspectors were all convinced that Hillside became more effective during the period of this study, most had an interest in the outcome and this may have influenced their judgement. In the claustrophobic environment of special measures, the inspect-ion process might have become circular, with HMI rewarding the school for implementing policies recommended by Ofsted, while governors and senior staff aimed to please the inspectors by follow-ing their advice. But this argument is undermined by the extent to which the relevant inspection criteria are based on effectiveness research and emphasise characteristics said to be linked with better performance. There is no reason to doubt that there was indeed a marked improvement in the characteristics believed to be signi-ficant for student achievement.

There is another quite different explanation for the lack of quanti-fiable improvement. The expectation of better results may simply be misplaced. Intake variables like social mix and relative dis-advantage may explain variations in test scores better than dif-ferences in perceived effectiveness (Thrupp, 1999). Few schools with disadvantaged intakes have produced a sustained improvement in results and this study shows how needy children can compromise performance figures. Is it surprising that Hillside's GCSE score was consistently within the range predicted by Ofsted (1998, p31) on the basis of the percentage eligible for free meals? GCSE results in the wards served by the school vary by post code in ways that suggest close links between poverty and low attainment (Easton Social Atlas). No direct link may exist between school characteristics and student outcomes. At Hillside, even a dramatic gain in perceived effectiveness seems to have made little difference to the results.

Recommendations

■ Government agencies should undertake a thorough review of policies based on the hypothesis that school improvement leads to better examination results. This case study adds to the growing evidence that social mix and disadvantage work in ways that can frustrate even the best school leaders. There is almost no evidence that most schools can change the pattern of their results.

Can leaders transform schools?

Although Hillside remained a relatively disadvantaged city school with below average results, the two consecutive new heads had clear transformational goals. Brian Goodlad, for example, invited teachers and students to commit themselves to a project larger than their private interests and goals (Burns, 1978) when he came in, and was open and positive with those who responded to his warmth and energy (Blase and Anderson, 1995). He told his colleagues they were involved in a struggle for survival that required exceptional action. He inspired parents, students and many of the teachers. He challenged accepted practices and galvanised the school for the campaign against special measures and closure.

Chris Moore's approach was even closer to the transforming or transformational (Bass, 1985) models of leadership, although he seldom operated in the democratic, empowering mode visualised by Blase and Anderson (1995). At Hillside leaders and followers did, at least to some extent, 'raise one another to higher levels of motivation and morality' (Burns, 1978, p20). Mr Moore aimed to 'elevate members' self-centred attitudes, values and beliefs' (Starratt, 1999, p25) and to build a new culture by passing through the transactional, transitional and transformational stages. Although he adopted micro-political tactics to deal with those who resisted change, many long-serving staff followed his lead and worked with remarkable intensity to save their school and recover their self-respect. Mr Moore's principled stance made possible the transformed culture identified by a visitor who found a 'tremendous buzz of people wanting new ideas'. Cultural change was 'effective and swift' (Torrington and Weightman, 1993, p53), mainly because so many teachers and students seized the opportunity to help reinvent their school.

The behaviour of the heads is plainly compatible with many of the descriptors used in the literature to describe transforming leadership. As Kotter (1996) recommends, the new heads:

- established a sense of urgency
- created a guiding coalition
- developed a vision and strategy
- communicated the change vision
- empowered broad-based action
- generated short-term wins
- consolidated gains and produced more change
- anchored approaches in the culture.

Mr Goodlad created an immediate sense of urgency and Mr Moore never allowed complacency to return. Mr Goodlad appointed a completely new senior management team, which Mr Moore used to develop the 'guiding coalition' that would implement and sustain the change programme. Senior management, parents and staff were powerful agents for transformation and ensured broad-based action. Both leaders used every vehicle of communication to reinforce their messages and mobilise the widest possible support. Within less than a year, new systems and procedures had become an established part of the culture, while the annual calendar of socials, festivals and celebrations indicates how an increasingly lively culture reflected the school's new values and goals.

Although no one has 'set out clearly and accurately' the general criteria for a 'successful programme of transformation' and critics are inclined to 'question the extent of the transformation that has taken place' (Dunford, 2002, p6), the depth and quality of change at Hillside deserves to be described in transformational terms. The school's effectiveness and capacity were greatly increased by:

- ◾ enhanced, better coordinated leadership at all levels

- ◾ well-articulated values and a culture of continuous improvement

- ◾ well-organised curriculum structures based on flexibility and entitlement

- ◾ capable, skilful teachers committed to improving the classroom experience for all students

- ◾ an intensive, needs-related programme of professional development.

Over the three years, four successive HMI monitoring and inspection reports charted a steady and eventually impressive improvement in the standards of teaching and learning. The evidence from Hillside suggests that leaders can directly enhance the quality of education, although social disadvantage seems to limit the extent to which such progress can be translated into measurably better results.

The critical question that remains is whether leaders can learn and apply the lessons of transformations like this so that all schools exceed our expectations. Should the Hillside example encourage the belief that leadership can transform the system or should we conclude that all improvement is a continuous struggle in which success depends on unique combinations of people and circumstances? The final chapter considers how we should ultimately view the Hillside transformation – was it an illusion or a reality?

8

Illusion or Reality?

Common sense

The story of Hillside shows that parents, children and teachers have great expectations of their leaders. Although the moralising paternalism of the headmaster tradition may have faded in these more democratic times, members of a school community still ascribe their successes, frustrations and failures to the larger-than-life characteristics of the man or woman in the principal's office. Followers' stories reveal through metaphor and myth the potency they attribute to the head's role in their affairs. Mr Wake's lunchtime chains were construed as a symbol of confinement and oppression; Mr Goodlad's decision to cut them down was a sign of promised freedom. The working assumption that head-teachers are the primary influence on the work, achievement and reputations of their schools is not confined to policy-makers and education researchers.

As we saw in chapter seven, the common sense belief that leaders make an important difference is confirmed by the marked contrast between Mr Wake and his successors. Albert Wake's disgruntled, pessimistic leadership permeated every aspect of school life and his unpredictable but often dismissive attitude made many teachers and students almost clinically miserable. Hillside lacked direction or purpose. Mr Wake rejected change and refused to adapt to the environment beyond the school. The impact on public and professional perceptions was cumulative. Local children transferred elsewhere; teachers realised that a move to Hillside would not enhance their careers.

Although change initiatives have often failed, the evidence is that some schools in special measures can be turned round with surprising speed (Stark, 1998). At Hillside the two new leaders introduced highly significant improvements. A positive climate was created almost immediately and new working practices were agreed and enforced. Basic management systems were introduced and made to work. The turbulence and demoralisation created by Ofsted and the threat of closure did not prove serious obstacles to progress. On the contrary, the emergency may have helped Mr Goodlad and Mr Moore by justifying their use of unorthodox and unfamiliar methods. Obstructive colleagues were swept aside and the school's culture was actively and deliberately re-engineered. The transformation was as swift and tangible as the change produced when a troublesome class is taken over by an experienced and capable teacher. Old habits do not disappear overnight, missing homework is not suddenly handed in – but attitudes and relationships are transformed and the students begin to respond to their teacher's expectations, some more quickly than others.

Public perceptions also changed rapidly. As soon as the threat of closure receded, Hillside began to recruit better qualified and more enthusiastic teachers. And the local primaries began to see the school as a natural choice. Hillside confirms, therefore, that experienced and effective heads can bring about rapid change, even in the most unpromising circumstances. The strategies adopted in this case study resemble those which seem to have worked elsewhere (Hopkins, 2000, Stark, 1998). Despite the school's successful transformation, however, Mr Moore recognised the limitations of the special measures regime and the strategies he had adopted. He noticed that the staff had learned to follow 'the formula' so that teaching had become 'convergent, much less user-friendly than it needed to be'. He sensed that his strong management style had discouraged the collegial and collaborative approaches he believed necessary for improvement to continue.

Lost ground had been made up, organisational health had been restored, but Mr Moore believed that a qualitatively different type of leadership was required to bring about further improvements in capacity and culture. He guessed that his colleagues would have to become more divergent and less docile if they were to transcend their past experiences and overcome the blight of social disadvantage. Exhausted by the struggle with Ofsted and the LEA, Mr Moore decided that he could not himself attempt such a transition. Instead, Hillside recruited its fourth headteacher in three years.

Frequent changes of head are a notable feature of struggling schools, especially of those entering and leaving special measures (McMahon, 2001, Stark, 1998). Leaders often leave after they have engineered important improvements, generating a lack of continuity that may explain the regression experienced by many schools emerging from special measures. A troublesome class requires sustained attention, not a short-lived rescue mission at the end of term. Leadership does make a difference.

The leadership models developed by the NCSL (2003) and the effectiveness criteria adopted by Ofsted and other government agencies (Sammons *et al*, 1995) help us to understand the differences between the heads at Hillside and help explain their contrasting impact on the school's progress. The analysis in chapter seven shows that although there are other, equally plausible, perspectives on leadership (Avolio and Bass, 1990), the models and criteria applied in the UK provide a well-grounded and valid framework for describing and evaluating school leadership and school improvement.

The transformational illusion
Our ability to analyse and synthesise the characteristics of effective leaders and effective schools has created the illusion that the example provided by a small number of high-performing heads can be generalised across the system. Policy-makers seem to believe that all schools can be transformed so as to achieve remarkable performance gains. But there are reasons why this is unlikely:

■ There are not enough good leaders to go round. (Ofsted, 2001)

■ A looming recruitment crisis threatens to reduce rather than increase the quality and supply of good leaders. (Hartle and Thomas, 2003)

■ Most senior managers in schools do not experience sustained leadership training. Levels of investment are not proportionate to what would be required to enable the average headteacher to perform at the standard of the best.

■ Current training models over-emphasise interpersonal skills that are difficult to develop, and seriously neglect the professional, moral and bureaucratic dimensions of leadership that are at least as important.

■ Leaders are unlikely to commit to the degree of personal change required to enable them to perform at a much higher level. There is evidence that heads resist change and are driven by well-established perceptions of how things should be done. (Argyris, 1991)

■ The common elements of successful leadership featured in official models are less significant than the differences produced by the infinite complications of people and circumstances. Generalisations based on surface similarities may mask important variations between cases. Advice from government agencies is likely to become less useful as leaders encounter a distinctive mixture of human problems and dilemmas. (Barker, 2003)

■ There is little evidence that leaders have a significant impact on test and examination results (Harris, 2004). Social disadvantage remains the most important determinant of school achievement.

Able leaders can make an important difference to the quality of organisational life. Parents, teachers and children tell us so. Schools can become richer and more fulfilling places when they are well led and managed and give everyone a chance to pursue success. As this study shows, we can compare and contrast our leaders, identifying the characteristics and qualities that please or frustrate us. But heads remain enigmatic and unpredictable. The awkward shaper (Belbin, 1981) is as likely to succeed as the smooth master or mistress of style. The moral and professional qualities required for wise government are not easily developed or generalised and we should not count upon a dramatic increase in the stock of gifted leaders or on everyone learning to be above average. Transformations are likely to remain rare and to be achieved by those fortunate combinations of leaders and followers who find themselves in the right place at the right time.

Appendix

Table 1: Ofsted Inspection Findings
Hillside was placed in special measures following the inspection

Key Characteristics of Effective Schools	Quotations from the Hillside School Ofsted Inspection Report
Professional Leadership	Weaknesses arise from serious shortcomings in the quality of leadership and management. There is a lack of awareness of the urgent need to link roles and responsibilities to the improvement of the school's effectiveness.
Shared Vision And Goals	Leadership does not take a strategic view. There are no effective strategic planning procedures so there are important weaknesses in the quality of planning and decision-making.
A Learning Environment	Pupils can become poorly behaved and restless. Teachers, by their attitude, provoke bad behaviour.
Concentration on Teaching and Learning	The low level of punctuality has an adverse effect on attainment and progress.
Purposeful Teaching	The quality of teaching varies widely across the school and this has an important impact on pupils' progress. A third of lessons are unsatisfactory or poor. Just over a quarter of lessons were judged to be good.
High Expectations	Leadership does not promote a positive ethos and high expectations. In many lessons, expectations are low and the pace of teaching is slow.

Key Characteristics of Effective Schools	Quotations from the Hillside School Ofsted Inspection Report
Positive Reinforcement	The school's provision for the development of pupils' spiritual, moral, social and cultural development is weak.
Monitoring Progress	Progress is judged to be unsatisfactory in almost 40% of lessons. The school does not evaluate its work systematically and does not have sufficient experience in the collection and evaluation of evidence.
Pupil Rights And Responsibilities	There are few opportunities for pupils to take responsibility for themselves or for others.
Home-School Partnership	There is a limited involvement of parents in the daily life of the school.
A Learning Organisation	The amount of staff development and contact with a range of sources of new ideas and expertise is low. There is no agreed staff development policy.

Table 2: HMI Inspection Findings
'Hillside no longer requires special measures'

Key Characteristics of Effective Schools	Quotations from the Hillside School Ofsted Inspection Report
Professional Leadership	The senior management team provides strong leadership and give clear direction. They have been successful in establishing a work ethic.
Shared Vision And Goals	The reformed and developing ethos of the school matches its aims. Progress is consistent across subjects.
A Learning Environment	The behaviour of pupils in classrooms is good. Pupils are generally orderly in their movement around the school, even in naturally congested areas.
Concentration on Teaching and Learning	The setting of homework is an integral part of curriculum planning and homework is well used to extend learning. Attendance rates have improved, although punctuality is a problem for a minority. Extra-curricular provision is a strength of the school.
Purposeful Teaching	The quality of teaching was sound or better in nine out of ten lessons, and in two out of five it was good. The structure of lessons is clear and teachers are increasingly using an appropriate range of teaching styles.
High Expectations	The headteacher has been resolute in his endeavour to improve teaching. Support to address weaknesses in teaching, and staff changes, have proved beneficial for continual overall improvement.
Positive Reinforcement	The pupils' moral and social development is good. There are clear and well-publicised guidelines for acceptable conduct.
Monitoring Progress	Individual pupil planners play an important part in monitoring pupils' progress. Marking and assessment support pupils' learning. The work of the school is monitored and evaluated in a systematic way and good practice is identified and disseminated to achieve further improvements.

Key Characteristics of Effective Schools	Quotations from the Hillside School Ofsted Inspection Report
Pupil Rights And Responsibilities	Pupils demonstrate a worthy sense of values and show respect for each others' views. The school has taken a number of initiatives to reflect and celebrate the multicultural nature of the school population.
Home-School Partnership	No comment.
A Learning Organisation	Staff have worked hard to improve the school. They feel valued and confident, and morale is high. The school has the capacity for self-improvement.

References

Allix, N. (2000) Transformational leadership, *Educational Management and Administration*, 28(1): 7-20

Angus, L. (2002) New leadership and the possibility of educational reform, in Smyth, J. ed, *op. cit.*

Argyris, C. (1991) Teaching smart people how to learn, *Harvard Business Review*, May-June: 99-109

Astuto, T. and Clark, D. (1986) Achieving effective schools, in Hoyle, E. and McMahon, A. eds, *op. cit.*

Avolio, B. and Bass, B. (1990) *The Full Range of Leadership Program: Basic and Advanced Manual*, NY: Bass, Avolio and Associates

Ball, S. (1981) *Beachside Comprehensive*, Cambridge: Cambridge University Press

Ball, S. (1987) *The Micro-Politics of the School*, London: Methuen

Barber, M. (1997) Re-engineering the political/educational system, *School Leadership and Management* 17(2): 187-199

Barber, M. (1998) The other side of the moon, in Stoll, L. and Myers, K. eds, *op. cit.*

Barker, B. (2001) Do Leaders Matter? *Educational Review,* 53(1): 65-76

Barker, B. (2003) Transforming Schools: Art, Science or Illusion? Leicester: Unpublished thesis submitted for the degree of PhD at the University of Leicester

Bass, B. (1985) *Leadership and Performance Beyond Expectations*, New York: Free Press

Bass, B. and Avolio, B. eds (1994) *Improving Organizational Effectiveness through Transformational Leadership*, Thousand Oaks: London: Sage Publications.

Bassey, M. (1999) *Case Study Research in Educational Settings*, Buckingham: Open University Press

Begley, P. (1999) Academic and practitioner perspectives on values, in Begley, P. and Leonard, P. eds, *op. cit.*

Begley, P. and Leonard, P. eds (1999) *The Values of Educational Administration*, London: Falmer Press

Belbin, M. (1981) *Management Teams: Why they succeed or fail*, London: Butterworth-Heinemann

Bell, L. (1988) The school as an organization: a reappraisal, in Westoby, A. ed, *op. cit.*

Bem, S. (1974) The measurement of psychological androgyny, *Journal of Consulting and Clinical Psychology*, 42(2): 155-62

Berg, L. (1968) *Risinghill: Death of a Comprehensive School*, Harmondsworth: Penguin Books

Bernstein, B. (1977) *Class, Codes and Control,* Vol. 3, London: Routledge

Blackmore, J. (1993) 'In the shadow of men': the historical construction of educational administration as a 'masculinist' enterprise, in Blackmore, J. and Kenway, J. eds, *op. cit.*

Blackmore, J. and Kenway, J. eds (1993) *Gender Matters in Educational Administration and Policy,* London: Falmer Press

Blair, T. (2001) Our schools can only get better if they are distinct, *The Times,* 14 February, p22.

Blase, J. and Anderson, G. (1995) *The Micropolitics of Educational Leadership,* London: Cassell

Blunkett, D. (2000) National College for School Leadership, Letter to Richard Greenhalgh, with list of tasks and responsibilities, London: DfEE

Bolam, R. (2004) Reflections on the NCSL from a historical perspective, *Educational Management Administration and Leadership,* 32(3): 251-267

Burgess, R. (1983) *Experiencing Comprehensive Education: A study of Bishop McGregor School,* London: Methuen

Burns, J. (1978) *Leadership,* New York: Harper Row

Calder, A. (1969) *The People's War: Britain 1939-45,* London: Jonathan Cape

Caldwell, B. and Spinks, J. (1992) *Leading the Self-Managing School,* London: Falmer Press

Carspecken, P. (1996) *Critical Ethnography in Educational Research,* New York and London: Routledge

Chitty, C. (1989) *Towards a New Education System: The Victory of the New Right?* London: Falmer Press

Clark, P. (1998) *Back from the Brink,* London: Metro Books

Coleman, M. ed. (1998) *Women in Educational Management,* Leicester: Educational Management Development Unit, University of Leicester

Collarbone, P. (2001) *Leadership Programme for Serving Headteachers: a review,* Nottingham: NCSL

Collins, J. (2001) *Good to Great,* New York: HarperCollins.

Covey, S. (1992) *Principle Centred Leadership,* London: Simon and Schuster

Creemers, B. (1994) The history, value and purpose of school effectiveness studies, in Reynolds, D. *et al.* eds, *op. cit.*

Cuban, L. (1988) *The Managerial Imperative and the Practice of Leadership in Schools,* Albany, NY: State University of New York Press

Cutler, V. (1991) St Paul's Way School, in Mortimore, P. and Mortimore, J. eds, *op. cit.*

Davies, B. and Hentschke, G. (1998) School autonomy: myth or reality – developing an analytical taxonomy, in Strain, M., Dennison, B., Ouston, J. and Hall, V. eds, *op. cit.*

Davies, N. (2000) *The School Report,* London: Vintage

Dawson, P. (1981) *Making a Comprehensive Work,* Oxford: Basil Blackwell

Day, C., Harris, A., Hadfield, M., Tolley, H. and Beresford, J. (2000) *Leading Schools in Times of Change,* Buckingham: Open University Press

Dennison, B. (1998) Education policy (1972-97): the emergence of the 'independent' school, in Strain, M., Dennison, B., Ouston, J. and Hall, V. eds, *op. cit.*

Denscombe, M. (1983) Interviews, accounts and ethnographic research on teachers, in Hammersley, M. ed, *op. cit.*

Department for Education and Employment (1997) *Excellence in Schools,* London: The Stationery Office

Department for Education and Employment (1998) *Target-setting in schools,* circular no. 11/98, London: Department for Education and Employment Publications

Doughty, J. (1998) The Changing Role of the Secondary Headteacher, Leicester: Unpublished thesis submitted for the degree of Doctor of Philosophy at the University of Leicester

Dunford, J. (2002) Transforming secondary schools? *Headlines,* (40), November: 6-8

Earley, P. and Evans, J. (2004) Making a difference? Leadership development for headteachers and deputies – ascertaining the impact of the National College for School Leadership, *Educational Management Administration and Leadership,* 32(3): 325-338

Earley, P. and Weindling, D. (2004) *Understanding School Leadership,* London: Paul Chapman Publishing

Evans, L. (1999) *Managing to Motivate,* London/New York: Cassell.

Evetts, J. (1994) *Becoming a Secondary Headteacher,* London: Cassell

Fidler, B. (2001) A structural critique of school effectiveness and school improvement, in Harris, A. and Bennett, N. eds, *op. cit.*

Fink, D. (1999) The attrition of change: A study of change and continuity, *School Effectiveness and School Improvement,* 10(3): 269-295

Fitz, J., Lee, J. and Eke, R. (2000) Inspection, regulation and governance: the role of school inspection under Labour, Cardiff: Paper prepared for the British Educational Research Association Conference, Cardiff University, 7-9 September

Fullan, M. (1982) *The Meaning of Educational Change,* New York: Teachers College Press

Fullan, M. (2000a) The return to large-scale reform, *Times Educational Supplement,* 23 June, p23.

Fullan, M. (2000b) The role of the head in school improvement, Background paper for the National College of School Leadership, June 2000 in *NCSL Leadership Evidence Base* @ www.ncsl.org.uk/index.cfm?pageid=ev_auth_fullan

Fullan, M. (2003) *The Moral Imperative of School Leadership,* Thousand Oaks, CA: Corwin Press

Giddens, A. (1991) *Modernity and Self-Identity,* Cambridge: Polity Press

Gold, A., Evans, J., Earley, P., Halpin, D., and Collarbone, P. (2003) Principled principals? Values-driven leadership: Evidence from ten case studies of 'outstanding' school leaders', *Educational Management and Administration,* 31(2): 127-137

Goleman, D., Boyatzis, R. and McKee, A. (2003) *The New Leaders: Transforming The Art of Leadership into the Science of Results,* London: Time Warner

Gomm, R., Hammersley, M. and Foster, P. (2000) Case study and generalization, in Gomm, R., Hammersley, M. and Foster, P. eds, *op. cit.*

Gomm, R., Hammersley, M. and Foster, P. eds (2000) *Case Study Method,* London: Sage

Grace, G. (1995) *School Leadership,* London: Falmer Press

Gray, J. and Wilcox, B. (1995) The inspectors recommended... a follow-up study in six secondary schools, in Gray, J. and Wilcox, B. eds, *op. cit.*

Gray, J. and Wilcox, B. eds (1995) *Good School, Bad School: Evaluating Performance and Encouraging Improvement,* Buckingham: Open University Press

Gray, J., Hopkins, D., Reynolds, D., Wilcox, B., Farrell, S., and Jesson, D. (1999) *Improving Schools: Performance and Potential,* Buckingham/Philadelphia: Open University Press

Gray, J., Jesson, D. and Sime, N. (1995) Estimating differences in examination performances of secondary schools in six LEAs: a multi-level approach to school effectiveness, in Gray, J. and Wilcox, B. eds, *op. cit.*

Greenfield, T. and Ribbins, P. eds (1993) *Greenfield on Educational Administration*, London: Routledge

Gronn, P. (1998) From transactions to transformations: a new world order in the study of leadership? in Strain, M., Dennison, B., Ouston, J. and Hall, V. eds, *op. cit.*

Gronn, P. (1999) *The Making of Educational Leaders*, London: Cassell

Gunter, H. (2001) *Leaders and Leadership in Education*, London: Paul Chapman

Hall, V. (1998) Women's approaches to management, in Coleman, M. ed, *op. cit.*

Hall, V., Mackay H. and Morgan, C. (1986) *Head Teachers at Work*, Milton Keynes: Open University Press

Hall, V. and Southworth, G. (1997) *Headship, School Leadership and Management*, 17(2): 151-170

Hammersley, M. ed. (1983) *The Ethnography of Schooling: Methodological Issues*, Driffield: Studies in Education Ltd, Nafferton Books.

Hampton, G. and Jones, J. (2000) *Transforming Northicote School: The reality of school improvement*, London: RoutledgeFalmer

Hargreaves, A. and Fink, D. (2001) Educational reform and school leadership in 3D perspective, *NCSL Leadership Evidence Base* @ www.ncsl.org.uk/index.cfm?pageid= ev_auth_hargreavesfink

Harris, A. (2001) Contemporary perspectives on school effectiveness and school improvement, in Harris, A. and Bennett, N. eds, *op. cit.*

Harris, A. (2004) Distributed leadership and school improvement – leading or misleading, in *Educational Management Administration and Leadership*, 32(1): 11-22

Harris, A. and Bennett, N. eds (2001) *School Effectiveness and School Improvement*, London: Continuum.

Harvard Business Review on Leadership (1998), Boston MA: Harvard Business School Press

Hartle, F. and Thomas, K. (2003) *Summary Report, Growing Tomorrow's School Leaders: the challenge*, Nottingham: National College for School Leadership

Haydon, G. ed (1987) *Education for a Pluralist Society*, London: Bedford Papers 30, London University Institute of Education

Hodgkinson, C. (1991) *Educational Leadership: The Moral Art*, Albany: State University of New York Press

Hodgkinson, C. (1993) Foreword, in Greenfield, T. and Ribbins, P. eds, *op. cit.*

Hopkins, D. (1984) What is school improvement? Staking out the territory? in Hopkins, D. and Wideen, M. eds, *op. cit.*

Hopkins, D. ed (1987) *Improving the Quality of Schooling: Lessons from the OECD International School Improvement Project*, Lewes: Falmer Press.

Hopkins, D. (2000) One size does not fit all, Paper given as part of the University of Keele-TES lecture series, 6 June

Hopkins, D. and Wideen, M. eds (1984) *Alternative Perspectives on School Improvement*, Lewes: Falmer Press

House of Commons (1999a) Education and Employment Committee, Fourth Report, *The Work of OFSTED*, Vol. I, Report and Proceedings of the Committee, London: The Stationery Office

House of Commons (1999b) Education and Employment Committee, Fourth Report, *The Work of OFSTED*, Vol. III, Appendices, London: The Stationery Office

Hoyle, E. and McMahon, A. eds. (1986) *The Management of Schools*, London: Kogan Page.

Hughes, M. (1998) Research report: the professional-as-administrator: the case of the secondary school head, in Strain, M., Dennison, B., Ouston, J. and Hall, V. eds, *op. cit.*

Jackson, B. and Marsden, D. (1962) *Education and the Working Class*, London: Routledge and Kegan Paul

Jencks, C., Smith, M., Ackland, H., Bane, M., Cohen, D., Grintis, H., Hegus, B. and Micholoson, N. (1972) *Inequality: A Reassessment of the Effect of Family and Schooling in America*, New York: Basic Books

Kotter, J. (1996) *Leading Change*, Boston, MA: Harvard Business School Press

Kruchov, C., MacBeath, J. and Riley, K. (1998) Introduction, in MacBeath, J. ed, *op. cit.*

Kuhn, T. (1975) *The Structure of Scientific Revolutions*, London: University of Chicago Press

Leithwood, K., Begley, P. and Bradley Cousins, J. (1992) *Developing Expert Leadership for Future Schools*, London: Falmer Press

Leithwood, K. and Jantzi, D. (2000) The effects of different sources of leadership on student engagement in school, in Riley, K. and Louis, K. eds, *op. cit.*

Leithwood, K., Rutherford, W. and van der Vegt, R. eds (1987) *Preparing School Leaders for Educational Improvement*, Beckenham: Croom Helm

Levačić, R. and Woods, P. (2002a) Raising school performance in the league tables (part 1): disentangling the effects of social disadvantage, *British Educational Research Journal*, 28(2): 207-226

Levačić, R. and Woods, P. (2002b) Raising school performance in the league tables (part 2): barriers to responsiveness in three disadvantaged schools, *British Educational Research Journal*, 28(2): 227-247

Litwin, G. and Stringer, R. (1968) *Motivation and Organizational Climate*, Boston: Division of Research, Graduate School of Business Administration, Harvard University

Lupton, R. (2004) Understanding local contexts for schooling and their implications for school processes and quality, BERA *Research Intelligence,* November 2004, (89)

MacBeath, J. ed. (1998) *Effective School Leadership: Responding to Change*, London: Paul Chapman

MacIntyre, A. (1993) *After Virtue*, London: Duckworth

Maden, M. ed (2001) *Success Against the Odds – Five Years On*, London: RoutledgeFalmer

McClelland, D. (1987) *Human Motivation,* New York: CUP

McClelland, D. and Burnham, D. (1995) Power is the great motivator, Boston, *Harvard Business Review*, January-February, Classic Reprint 95108, originally published in March-April 1976: 100-110

McMahon, A. (2001) Fair Furlong Primary School, in Maden, M. ed, *op. cit.*

McNeil, L. (2000) *Contradictions of School Reform, Educational Costs of Standardised Testing,* New York: Routledge

Mintzberg, H. (1975) The manager's job: folklore and fact, *Harvard Business Review,* July-August, reproduced in *Harvard Business Review on Leadership* (1998), *op. cit.*

Mortimore, P. and Mortimore, J. eds (1991) *The Secondary Head: Roles, Responsibilities and Reflections*, London: Paul Chapman

Mortimore, P. and Whitty, G. (2000) *Can school improvement overcome the effects of disadvantage?* London: Institute of Education University of London (1st edn 1997)

National College for School Leadership (2001) *Leadership Development Framework,* Nottingham: NCSL @ www.ncsl.org.uk

National College for School Leadership (2003) *Leadership Programme for Serving Headteachers: Facilitator Guide,* Nottingham: NCSL

Office for Standards in Inspection (1999) *Broadsheet,* Hexham: Ofstin Working Group

Ofsted (1994) *Review of Action Plans,* London: HMSO

Ofsted (1998) *The Annual Report of Her Majesty's Chief Inspector of Schools 1996/97,* London: The Stationery Office

Ofsted (2001) Leadership in schools, in *NCSL Leadership Evidence Base* @ www.ncsl.org.uk/index.cfm?pageid=ev_auth_OFSTED

Ozga, J. ed (1993) *Women in Educational Management,* Buckingham: Open University Press

Peters, T. (1989) *Thriving on Chaos,* London: Pan Books

Peters, T. and Waterman, R. (1995) *In Search of Excellence,* London: Harper and Row (1st edn 1982)

Pitner, N. (1987) Administrator preparation in the United States, in Leithwood, K, Rutherford, W. and van der Vegt, R. eds, *op. cit.*

Preedy, M. ed (1993) *Managing the Effective School,* London: Open University/Paul Chapman

Pring, R. (2000) *Philosophy of Educational Research,* London: Continuum

Reynolds, D. *et al.* eds (1994) *Advances in School Effectiveness Research and Practice,* Oxford: Pergamon

Ribbins, P. and Sherratt, B. (1997) *Radical Educational Policies and Conservative Secretaries of State,* London: Cassell

Riley, K. and Louis, K. eds (2000) *Leadership for Change and School Reform,* London/New York: RoutledgeFalmer

Riley, K. and MacBeath, J. (1998) Effective leaders and effective schools, in MacBeath, J. ed, *op. cit.*

Rutter, M., Maugham, B., Mortimore, P. and Ouston, J. (1979) *Fifteen Thousand Hours: Secondary Schools and their Effects on Children,* London: Open Books

Sammons, P., Hillman, J. and Mortimore, P. (1995) *Key Characteristics of Effective Schools: A review of school effectiveness research,* London Ofsted/Institute of Education

Schein, E. (2004) *Organisational Culture and Leadership,* San Francisco, CA: Jossey-Bass

School Management Task Force (1990) *Developing School Management,* London: HMSO

Sergiovanni, T. (1995) *The Principalship,* Boston: Allyn and Bacon.

Shakeshaft, C. (1998) Differences between the ways women and men manage schools, in Coleman, M. ed, *op. cit.*

Smiles, S. (1860) *Self-Help: with illustrations of Character and Conduct,* London: John Murray

Smyth, J. ed (2002) *Critical Perspectives on Educational Leadership,* London: RoutledgeFalmer

Stark, M. (1998) No slow fixes either, in Stoll, L. and Myers, K. eds, *op. cit.*

Starratt, R. (1999) Moral dimensions of leadership, in Begley, P. and Leonard, P. eds, *op. cit.*

Stoll, L. and Fink, D. (1995) *Changing Our Schools: Linking school effectiveness and school improvement,* Buckingham: Open University Press

Stoll, L. and Myers, K. (1998) Introduction, in Stoll, L. and Myers, K. eds, *op. cit.*

Stoll, L. and Myers, K. eds (1998) *No Quick Fixes,* London: Falmer Press

Strain, M., Dennison, B., Ouston, J. and Hall, V. eds (1998) *Policy, Leadership and Professional Knowledge in Education,* London: Paul Chapman Publishing

Tannen, D. (1996) *Talking From 9 to 5,* London: Virago

Taylor, F. (1911) *The Principles of Scientific Management,* New York: Harper

Teacher Training Agency (2001) *National Standards for Headteachers,* London: TTA

Thrupp, M. (1999) *Schools Making A Difference: Let's Be Realistic,* Buckingham-Philadelphia: Open University Press

Torrington, D. and Weightman, J. (1993) 'The culture and ethos of the school', in Preedy, M. ed, *op. cit.*

Van Velzen, W. (1987) The International School Improvement Project, in Hopkins, D. ed, *op. cit.*

Weber, M. (1964) *The Theory of Social and Economic Organizations,* trans. Henderson, A. and Parsons, T., New York: The Free Press (1st published 1947, Oxford University Press)

Weick, K. (1988) Educational organizations as loosely coupled systems, in Westoby, A. ed, *op. cit.*

West, M., Jackson, D., Harris, A. and Hopkins, D. (2000) Learning through leadership, leadership through learning: leadership for sustained school improvement, in Riley, K. and Louis, K. eds, *op. cit.*

West, S. (1991) Values and the arts, in *All-In Success, Journal of the Centre for the Study of Comprehensive Schools,* 3(5): 26-28

West, S. (1993) *Educational Values for School Leadership,* London: Kogan Page

Westoby, A. ed (1988) *Culture and Power in Educational Organizations,* Milton Keynes: Open University Press

White, J. (1987) The quest for common values, in Haydon, G. ed, *op. cit.*

Wilson, B. and Corcoran, T. (1988) *Successful Secondary Schools: Visions of Excellence in American Public Education,* London: Falmer

Wolcott, H. (1984) *The Man In The Principal's Office,* Illinois: Waveland Press (1st edn 1973)

Yin, R. (1994) *Case Study Research. Design and Methods,* London: Sage

Index